Jackie Robinson

THE LIBRARY OF AFRICAN AMERICAN BIOGRAPHY

General Editor, John David Smith
Charles H. Stone Distinguished Professor of American History
University of North Carolina at Charlotte

The Library of African American Biography aims to provide concise, readable, and up-to-date lives of leading black figures in American history, in widely varying fields of accomplishment. The books are written by accomplished scholars and writers, and reflect the most recent historical research and critical interpretation. Illustrated with photographs, they are designed for general informed readers as well as for students.

Jackie Robinson: An Integrated Life, J. Christopher Schutz (2016)
W. E. B. Du Bois: An American Intellectual and Activist, Shawn Leigh Alexander (2015)
Paul Robeson: A Life of Activism and Art, Lindsey R. Swindall (2013)
Ella Baker: Community Organizer of the Civil Rights Movement, J. Todd Moye (2013)
Booker T. Washington: Black Leadership in the Age of Jim Crow, Raymond W. Smock (2010)
Walter White: The Dilemma of Black Identity in America, Thomas Dyja (2010)
Richard Wright: From Black Boy to World Citizen, Jennifer Jensen Wallach (2010)
Louis Armstrong: The Soundtrack of the American Experience, David Stricklin (2010)

Jackie Robinson

An Integrated Life

J. Christopher Schutz

ROWMAN & LITTLEFIELD
Lanham • Boulder • New York • London

Published by Rowman & Littlefield
A wholly owned subsidary of The Rowman & Littlefield Publishing Group, Inc.
4501 Forbes Boulevard, Suite 200, Lanham, Maryland 20706
www.rowman.com

Unit A, Whitacre Mews, 26-34 Stannary Street, London SE11 4AB

British Library Cataloguing in Publication Information Available

Library of Congress Cataloging-in-Publication Data

Names: Schutz, J. Christopher.
Title: Jackie Robinson : an integrated life / J. Christopher Schutz.
Description: Lanham, Maryland : Rowman & Littlefield, [2016] | Includes
    bibliographical references and index.
Identifiers: LCCN 2015042871| ISBN 9781442245969 (cloth : alk. paper) | ISBN
    9781442245976 (electronic)
Subjects: LCSH: Robinson, Jackie, 1919–1972. | Baseball players—United
    States—Biography. | African American baseball players—Biography. |
    Racism in sports—United States—History. | Discrimination in
    sports—United States—History. | Baseball—United States—History.
Classification: LCC GV865.R6 S355 2016 | DDC 796.357092—dc23 LC record available
    at http://lccn.loc.gov/2015042871

♾ ™ The paper used in this publication meets the minimum requirements of American
National Standard for Information Sciences—Permanence of Paper for Printed Library
Materials, ANSI/NISO Z39.48-1992.

Printed in the United States of America

To Colleen,
whose love and support have made everything possible,
and to Johnny Wright

Contents

Introduction

For nearly seventy years, the image of Jackie Robinson has been frozen in place as the compliant warrior, just happy to be here: in the white Major Leagues, in the mainstream of American society, in the welcoming arms of whites. His success has been trumpeted as "our success," a show of just how open America can be to African Americans. And Robinson, the story goes, did it the "right way": his Christlike willingness to bear modestly the sins of white America without striking back won it over and taught us all a lesson in humility and bravery.

The story, entombed in its comforting simplicity, reassures in just the same way as oversimplified portrayals told of Dr. King (which omit King's challenges to the Vietnam War and unfettered capitalism). This defanged, sunnier depiction of the baseball great serves as white America's antidote to its equally simplistic memory of angry blacks dominating the streets and headlines of the late 1960s.

The truth is that such a quiet, yielding Robinson might never have made it to the Major Leagues. From his earliest years, he was a determined, feisty, unrepentant young black man unwilling to scrape and bow to reach the top. His path to the Major Leagues might have been cut short in a youth characterized by dalliances with a street gang and tangles with police. The privileges accorded him as a local sports phenomenon saved him on more than one occasion from jail time. Even his athletic teammates could find him prickly and difficult and overly competitive.

His unwillingness to accept whites' limitations was the very ingredient that allowed him to succeed in the decidedly harsh world he entered alone. He did manage to endure the full brunt of white supremacy without returning it, but this image of the popular black baseball star gave way to his later

1

years in the game as a combative player who rankled—so much so that one notable article's title queried "Why They Boo Jackie Robinson."

Robinson's story also mirrors the narrative of African American history. His breakthrough in the Major Leagues illuminates the shifting landscape on race due to the World War II experience. African American soldiers, having responded to the highest call of their country, were equally determined to fight for their civil rights. Robinson's confrontation with authority during the war both continued his penchant for defying white supremacy and reflected the general impatience in American black communities with the status quo.

By the end of the war, the more racially progressive whites grew increasingly uncomfortable with the hypocrisies of trumpeting American freedom amid domestic segregation, but they were undeniably committed that any racial advancement arrive in a cautious, controlled manner. The emphasis on Robinson as a nonthreatening figure was thus made necessary by the anxieties of white liberals, cautious to go too far too fast.

The resulting "great experiment" of Robinson's arrival in the Majors would actually be greeted with far less warmth by many more whites than the nation has the courage to remember. Even more viewed Robinson's outspokenness and aggression in his later years in the game (after adhering to Dodgers president Branch Rickey's directive not to return attacks) as an unwelcome betrayal of whites' gift of acceptance. This more defiant Robinson revealed his true character, however, and was merely a harbinger of the uncomfortable years that lay around the corner in the civil rights movement.

Also complicated is the tale of baseball's integration itself. The journey was a much bumpier, difficult ride than whites' celebratory memories of opening the turnstiles fully to black baseball players. The story is rife with white reluctance and hostility, and numerous African American casualties left behind—including both legendary black athletes deemed too old when the moment finally presented itself, and the losses of many beloved Negro League teams that could not go on amid white teams' pilfering of their best players.

Through it all, Robinson was a man who defied expectations. His refusal to accept Jim Crow standards left him constantly searching for more in his early life, clashing at times with authorities. In the Negro Leagues, his repeated impatience with segregation even irritated some of his black teammates. In his first few years in the white Major Leagues, he battled racist stereotypes to succeed. For most of his years in the Majors that followed, he refused to be merely grateful for his "permitted" rise into the white world of professional sports.

His postbaseball years are marked by forays into civil rights issues and politics. As momentum for societal racial progress grew in the late 1950s and 1960s, he continued to play a role in the issue he had helped catalyze. A highly sought-after spokesman and fund-raiser for the cause, he brought the same outspokenness that defined most of life—including public criticism of the iconic National Association for the Advancement of Colored People (NAACP). As black, urban voices grew into the Black Power Movement by the mid- to late 1960s, his views resisted easy categorization as he both critiqued and supported the Black Power agenda at alternating moments.

In the political realm, Robinson used his sports popularity to push political figures to produce racial progress. Those concerns led him ever deeper into politics, where he worked on several different presidential campaigns (on both sides of the partisan aisle) and joined the gubernatorial staff of the prominent New York liberal Republican Nelson Rockefeller. Those years in politics shadow the important 1960s political transformations of the major parties. They also show a Robinson still determined, still chafing against expectations—in this case, that he hew to monolithic assumptions that a black man must support the Democratic Party. His resistance to being boxed into standard black political allegiances made him all too willing to shift course from one party to another—with the intent of finding a place where African Americans might leverage their power into real influence in the marketplace of political ideas.

His life stands as a visible challenge to the premise that a black man could not live the same full-blooded complexities allowed a white. Despite the frequently frozen image of Jack Roosevelt Robinson, his life and legacy eludes attempts to confine him just as surely as he evaded opponents' grasps in his Hall of Fame career.

CHAPTER ONE

Before the Legend

The Young Robinson

"My grandfather was born into slavery," Jackie Robinson later wrote, "and although my mother and father . . . lived during an era when physical slavery had been abolished, they also lived in a newer, more sophisticated kind of slavery," as sharecroppers in the sugarcane-growing region of southern Georgia. For Robinson's mother, things worsened considerably in the summer of 1919, when her husband, Jerry Robinson, left his sharecropping plot on Jim Sasser's plantation. He was going, he told his wife, Mallie, to visit his brother in Texas, but Mallie rightly feared that he was really leaving with one of his numerous extramarital paramours to parts unknown. His five-month-old son, Jack Roosevelt Robinson, never saw his father again.

Mallie remained behind with her five children and a meager sharecropping cabin. Her one asset was a steely determination that made for—in the words of a disgruntled Sasser—"about the sassiest nigger woman ever on this place." Her frequent agitation against the limitations of the plantation's restrictions (especially the decidedly unfavorable financial terms of her life there) made her presence increasingly unwelcome. Less than a year later, when she had had her fill of Sasser's white supremacist hospitality and mounting racist violence left local black churches and her hopes for a better life in ashes, she fled to the warmer racial clime of California.

On what Mallie called the "freedom train," she arrived in Pasadena, California, in the summer of 1920 with her children and $3 sewn into her petticoat. She moved in with her half-brother Burton Thomas, and later shared a house with her sister and brother-in-law. While racism was certainly milder in California than in her Deep South roots, the move hardly brought her "closer to heaven," as promised by Thomas before the move. Pasadena carefully restricted its black population from a number of public venues and services, from segregated movie theaters to groceries barring black customers. The public swimming pool, for example, was only open to African Americans one day per week (and only that after protests forced the concession). To reassure white Pasadenans, however, public workers drained and refilled the pool entirely after each of those weekly occasions. More problematic for Mallie Robinson were the job restrictions with which she was already all too familiar. Hoping for more, she was forced to accommodate herself to the traditional role for a black woman—domestic work. Although the pay and treatment were better than what she had left behind, Jackie recalls that the job, plus some help from welfare funds, "barely enabled her to make ends meet. Sometimes there were only two meals a day, and some days we wouldn't have eaten at all" if not for her domestic family's leftovers. Some days, the Robinsons ate only "bread and sweet water."

Her family's arrival in their mostly white neighborhood was less than welcome. Mallie's daughter Willa Mae remembers going "through a sort of slavery" at the Pepper Street home "with the whites slowly, very slowly, getting used to us." The children endured both epithets and rocks, and young Jackie Robinson returned both. "The police were there every other day" responding to white neighbors' complaints about the Robinson children, Jackie's sister recalls. In a physical reminder of the community's racial restrictions, the white officers left orders for the kids to remain in their own yard. Their home was subject to vandalism and a cross burning. Jackie's older brother Mack Robinson recounts that, faced with the repeated confrontations, "We just kicked some white ass. Kids aren't so tough when you can knock them down with a punch."

Jackie's obvious athletic aptitude from an early age, however, did win some reluctant respect. Besides his clear physical talent, another attribute he would carry throughout his life was evident from the beginning: a potent competitive streak. The latter did not always produce warm regards among his peers. "Jackie wasn't a very likable person," remembers one childhood friend, "because his whole thing was just win, win, win, and beat everybody." The attention he garnered for his sports acumen also made him lax in his studies, causing one friend to reflect that he "wasn't worth a damn" as a student.

Given Mallie's long hours, the older Robinson children were called on for parental roles. The siblings referred to eldest son Edgar informally as "Papa," but it was Willa Mae Robinson that shouldered the most responsibility for her young brother Jackie. Daily feeding, bathing, and dressing him, she was Jackie's "little mother." That even extended to her school hours. Kindly teachers allowed her brother to play in a sandbox outside the classroom window while eight-year-old Willa Mae kept whatever watchful eye she could during her lessons.

But his young siblings could not, of course, provide an adequate substitute for proper parental supervision. His resulting ample free time was sometimes used productively with a paper route and small jobs. "The rest of the time," Jackie later admitted, "I stole—all sorts of small things from stores." He also joined the neighborhood Pepper Street Gang, which caused "hardly a week" to go by without him visiting with the police. The gang's activities included hurling rocks at passing cars, knocking out street lamps, smashing windows, tarring the lawn of a racist neighbor, and pilfering stray balls at a golf course for resale. "[A]ll the time, we were aware," asserts Robinson, "of a growing resentment at being deprived of some of the advantages the white kids had."

At times, the young Robinson took a more direct approach to the racism that hindered him, violating a movie theater's segregated seating and even engaging in an impromptu sit-in at a local department store with a friend. "We were sitting in and we didn't even know what the hell we were doing," a friend sums up. As for the city's ordinance restricting swimming to one day per week for blacks, Jackie and his cohorts willfully swam in the municipal reservoir on a regular basis. When police caught wind of this, they surrounded the youngsters with guns drawn, one of them shouting, "Looka there—niggers swimming in my drinking water!" Robinson and fifteen of his friends were brought to the station for questioning. After four hours, one warned that the cumulative heat might cause him to faint. The officers responded by playing to stereotype, distributing watermelon and humiliatingly photographing the young thirsty blacks' desperate devouring of the fruit. Robinson called the experience "the most humiliating day of my life."

Adding to Jackie's bitterness was his brother Mack's experience. A phenomenal athlete in his own right, track and field was Mack Robinson's particular strength. Overcoming a diagnosed heart murmur as a young man, he set a junior high school hurdles record that had stood for more than twenty-five years. In 1936, he traveled to Berlin for the now famous challenge to Adolf Hitler's Aryan supremacy claims at the Olympics. Using the summer games as a showcase for his Nazi regime, the Führer was chastened by African American sprinter Jesse Owens's capturing of four gold medals. After Owens took the one-hundred-meter race, Hitler angrily and visibly left the stadium before the awards ceremony. Told later about the leader's snubbing, Owens responded, "It was all right with me. I didn't go to Berlin to shake hands with him, anyway. All I know is that I'm here now, and Hitler isn't." One of Owens's four gold medals might have gone to Mack Robinson (in the two hundred meters) had he not made the fatal mistake of looking over his shoulder in the final stretch. Instead, Mack toured Europe triumphantly with a silver medal.

America, however, accorded him a decidedly different reception. "There were no ticker-tape parades, no plaques, no nothing," Mack lamented. In fact, the track team was segregated into different hotels on the first night back in the United States. Having no contact with Hitler, he even noted that he was "treated very well" by average Germans by comparison to his home country. The silver medalist settled into a job as a street sweeper on the night shift. Pasadeneans could see him often wearing his leather U.S. Olympic jacket and a broom. Mack's fate left an indelible imprint on his younger brother, Jackie.

As Jackie's street life continued, even he admitted being in danger of becoming "a full-fledged juvenile delinquent." Two figures arrived to provide a kind of substitute paternal guidance at a critical time. Amid the heroic efforts of his mother to hold the family together, Robinson rarely addressed the loss of his father's presence at a young age. Nevertheless, it left a mark of nagging pain. "I could only think of him with bitterness. He, too, may have been a victim of oppression," he reflected, "but he had no right to desert my mother and five children." The void appears to have left him in a lifelong search for surrogates (Brooklyn Dodgers president Branch Rickey being the most prominent example). Carl Anderson was a car mechanic, local black scout leader, and important youth leader in the area who provided a guiding hand in Jackie's teen years. More important was Robinson's new young pastor, Karl Downs. Downs checked in with local authorities to identify troubled youth (which certainly included young Jackie Robinson) and lured them to his church for sports activities and a sympathetic ear. It was a place, said a friend, where Robinson "could always go to get straightened out." "To a fatherless boy," Jackie's future wife, Rachel, claims, "Karl offered not only a spiritual awakening but also a sense of direction." In time, Jack became one of Downs's Sunday school teachers and a lifelong friend.

If Robinson struggled to steer clear of trouble on the streets, he was in full command on the athletic field from an early age. "Sports," he later wrote, "were the big breach in the wall of segregation about me." Mastering virtually every sport he dabbled in (and he dabbled in many), he excelled in his high school's baseball, basketball, football, and track and field teams. His race limited many colleges' interest (either because administrators or coaches harbored prejudice and/or because they worried that their current players would), but he was lured by the local Pasadena Junior College (PJC) to continue his athletic exploits in early 1937. (Even the PJC football coach had to overcome a near boycott by several football players who objected to Robinson's presence.)

The school would not be disappointed. For his two years there, he starred on a football squad that lost only two games. He was the best player in his basketball team's conference. He led the baseball team to a conference championship. On a landmark day in 1938, he set the national junior college Amateur Athletic Union broad jump record (ironically breaking his brother Mack's previous mark). Then jumping into a friend's car, he drove forty miles to join his college baseball team midgame in a crucial division win.

As his two years at Pasadena Junior College were winding down, the scholarship offers from four-year schools stacked up. So significant was he regarded that Robinson claimed that a Stanford University alumnus actually offered to pay his tuition at any school outside Stanford's conference. Robinson's choices, though, were circumscribed. First was the reality of his race. Some schools would simply not be interested in breaching the color line with even an immensely talented black athlete like Robinson. More receptive institutions would worry about the scheduling limitations of other schools' refusal to play an integrated team. Jackie—still shy despite his aggressive sports demeanor—also resisted moving far from family to attend a university. This left the University of California at Los Angeles (UCLA) as the obvious choice, which eagerly recruited black athletes—mostly due to its determination to catch up to regional competitors.

Before he could begin his spectacular stint at UCLA college athletics, however, two sobering events threatened to derail his promising future. The summer before his first full semester of studies at UCLA, his older brother Frank suffered a fatal motorcycle accident. Frank Robinson had become an important source of paternal influence and support to Jackie, and he was a reliable spectator at Jackie's sporting events. He suffered miserably in his final hours, and losing him left the younger brother "very shaken." Without the benefit of Frank's guidance, perhaps it was not surprising that Jackie seemed to steer unnervingly toward his past habits on the streets that September, just before the college football season got underway.

Driving home with several friends from a softball game, a white motorist jeering them as "niggers" pulled up at a stoplight. Robinson's friend and football teammate, Ray Bartlett, struck him across the face with his ball glove in retaliation, causing the man to pull over angrily. Robinson immediately screeched in behind. Bartlett anticipated a fight between himself and the white offender, "[b]ut Jack got right in the middle of it, as usual." A crowd of forty to fifty blacks began to gather, and Bartlett thought the better of going further with the confrontation. "But not Jack," he regretted. "He just kept at it, you couldn't stop him." Just as the white man began to retreat, a white patrolman arrived and apparently felt rattled in the growing throng of young blacks. As he reached for his gun, one of Robinson's friends blocked his hand on the holster, urging him to relent. Amid the confusion—or possibly because Robinson also interceded in some way—Robinson became the target of the officer's now withdrawn gun. "I found myself up against the side of my car with a gun-barrel pressed unsteadily into the pit of my stomach," he later recounted. "I was scared to death."

Robinson soon found himself in the back of a patrol car facing a night in jail and charges for resisting arrest and hindering traffic. Surely affecting his demeanor toward police was his brother Edgar's unsettling police encounter several months prior. Beaten by two policemen as he awaited the arrival of Pasadena's signature annual Tournament of Roses parade, he was hauled in on resisting arrest and violating a city ordinance requiring a paid permit to bring chairs to the parade route. Had the officers not beaten him first, Edgar Robinson might have retrieved his receipt proving he had indeed paid for the chair. Denied medical treatment or a phone call at the station, he felt forced to plead guilty and pay his fine. After city hospital officials refused him treatment, he later attempted to lodge a police complaint. At the urging of the police chief, however, he decided to withdraw the complaint "before you are clubbed on the head." It was an experience all too common for black men, who were forced to resign themselves to regular police brutality and discriminatory justice.

With this firsthand knowledge of Pasadena "justice," a nervous Jackie also had a suspended sentence hanging over him from a year-and-a-half-old arrest. The record of that earlier conviction is muddled. Apparently an officer had taken offense to Robinson and a friend's boisterous singing of a suggestive song late one evening. When Robinson flouted proper deference to the white official (made more necessary by his race), he found himself spending the night in jail. Perhaps due to Jackie's sports acclaim, the judge had been lenient, making his ten-day sentence suspended (on the condition that he avoid arrest for two years).

Heightening Robinson's concern in his new predicament, he was denied the opportunity for a phone call. Only because his friends knew of the arrest was anyone contacted to assist him. His former junior college baseball coach paid Jackie's bond, but not before unleashing his exasperation on the friend contacting him about the talented young man who seemed to struggle staying on the right path. "What the hell is Jack doing this time?" he vented. "What's he in jail for?"

Now free, however, Robinson would enjoy the unique blessings offered a young black male with his athletic notoriety. A UCLA loyalist described in newspaper accounts merely as "an attorney prominent in sports circles in the state" contacted local officials, who permitted Robinson to forfeit bail and switch his plea to guilty. This would allow the judge to operate more leniently, including the mere payment of a small fine and the mysterious disappearance of his looming suspended sentence. The determining factor for the judicial compassion, said newspapers, had been insiders' request "that the Negro football player be not disturbed during the football season." Even Robinson knew "I got out of that trouble because I was an athlete." He never forgot this encounter "with bigotry of the meanest sort," nor the reputation created by the resulting press accounts. One especially painful headline compared his considerably elusive skills on the field to slipping out of the justice system's clutches: "Gridiron Phantom Lives Up to Name." "This thing followed me all over and it was pretty hard to shake off," he lamented.

With the legal danger averted, Robinson began his sterling career as a college athlete at UCLA in the fall of 1939—one of only about thirty blacks among several thousand students. His quickly visible talent even caused the athletic director concern. "He was so good at everything," he worried, "I was afraid our four coaches would start fighting among themselves." Robinson joined a football squad that had just made its first bowl game appearance the previous season, and returned two star players that fall: halfback Kenny Washington and receiver Woody Strode. Together, this so-called Gold Dust Trio carried the team to an undefeated record for the first time in its history. Although Washington's considerable fame and seniority limited the carries for the younger runner, Robinson's impact was immediately evident. Local journalists heralded Jackie's "hip-jiggling feints" and "blinding speed," which left defenders constantly in his wake. *Los Angeles Examiner* sportswriter Vincent Flaherty named Robinson "the Jim Thorpe of his race" (evoking the memory of the renowned Native American Olympic gold medalist and multiple sport legend of the early twentieth century). Opponents, too, were left speechless. Stanford's coach called him "the greatest backfield runner" he had seen in his twenty-five years in the ranks. A local paper cited University of Washington players as "unanimous in their statements that Robinson is the greatest thing they have ever seen."

But Robinson was only beginning, as he was to become UCLA's first four-sport letterman. He became the leading conference scorer in basketball. "If Jackie hadn't played football," claimed his coach, "he might have been the greatest of all basketball players." He won the national broad jump title in track and field, and set a conference record in the event as well. Ironically, his stint in a UCLA baseball uniform brought the most meager results, compiling a dispiriting 0.97 batting average.

Robinson continued to shine in the following season of UCLA athletics, although the teams surrounding him declined. The football team lost not only Washington and Strode but also their more experienced offensive linemen, making Jackie's job of breaking to running daylight much more difficult. They finished the 1940 campaign with a 1–9 record, despite his laudable efforts. The same narrative unfolded for basketball. Robinson may have won his division's scoring title, but the reduced supporting cast dragged the team down to only two of twelve conference wins.

By March 1941, Robinson had used up his athletic eligibility in football and basketball and was ready to move on. Against the counsel of coaches, his mother, and his girlfriend, Rachel Isum (later to be his wife), he withdrew from college without completing his degree. He worried about his mother's financial hardships, and remained "convinced that no amount of education would help a black man get a job. I felt I was living in an academic and athletic dream world."

Waiting for him was a job with the National Youth Administration (NYA), one of the array of New Deal programs created to battle the subsiding Great Depression. He hoped this would launch a more realistic career for him as an athletic director. Placed at a youth camp on the central California coast, his job was to organize sports activities for the impoverished young adults and teens targeted by the NYA (which hoped to improve their job prospects). Robinson quickly saw the path of his own youth mirrored in the youthful faces. "I realized that I had been no different than many of these kids," he later told an interviewer, "who would make good if given half a chance." Many had had it "pretty tough." Some, he grieved, "don't know anything about anything."

After only a few months, however, the camp was shuttered, as the nation's attention and budgetary priorities shifted to the growing war abroad. By the early fall, Robinson was on his way to Hawaii to play for the semiprofessional Honolulu Bears football organization. The offer came with a $100-per-game paycheck and a construction job offer during the daylight hours. Discontent quickly set in, first with the construction job, which a teammate recalled was short-lived since "Jack didn't like to work. . . . He'd pick up one board—not heavy—and put it on his shoulder, and carry it over to the carpenter. Finally the foreman said, 'Jack, in the future, I want you to pick up two boards at a time, okay?' Jack didn't last long on the job. Either he quit or was fired." His nighttime gridiron gig, of course, went dramatically better, until he suffered an injury at midseason and played on an injured ankle the rest of the way.

In early December, he had had enough. He boarded the S.S. *Lurline* for his southern California home. Robinson looked out over the ship railing, watching the brief good fortune and opportunities he had enjoyed as a black athlete disappearing behind him. His life and direction seemed just as adrift as the steamship that carried him.

CHAPTER TWO

Freedom Fighter

Aboard the *Lurline*, Robinson bided time by playing poker. His injury-aborted stint in Hawaiian professional football now over, he longed for better cards and a surer future. The poker players' quiet conversation was suddenly broken by crewmembers, who had hurriedly taken to painting the windows black and calling all passengers to the deck. The city Robinson had left two days ago had been bombed by Japanese war pilots. In the unsettling "new normal" after the Pearl Harbor attack, the ship traveled in blackout, often avoiding regular sea lanes to allude enemy detection. The captain handed out life jackets to all passengers. They were to wear them at all times now, in the event of a submarine assault.

Robinson later safely returned to the city of Los Angeles, a romance with Rachel Isum, and a truck driver job at a Lockheed defense plant. This was a Jackie Robinson still biding time, still looking to make his mark in a white man's world. In late March 1942, two events presaged his path for the coming years. One was a tryout at the Pasadena training facility of the Major League white baseball club, the Chicago White Sox. He was one of only two African American players invited. The other was pitcher Nate Moreland, who had already played some ball in the Negro Leagues and Mexico. Though White Sox manager Jimmy Dykes expressed some tantalizing interest—particularly in Robinson—nothing came of it. That was a track obviously waiting down the road for Robinson.

Much closer to his future laid a military draft notice. Robinson had officially listed himself in Selective Service papers as the sole means of support for his aging mother. Doing so previously would have lessened his chance of induction (and allowed him to support his mother more ably), but now, with the smoke of Pearl Harbor still drifting over the minds of Americans, such claims accounted for far less consideration. His effort at the earlier draft exemption (by listing the family economic hardship) no doubt also reflected a reluctance shared by many other young blacks to support the war effort fully.

The harsh memories about African American veterans' fates in the months after World War I had hardly healed over by the dawn of the next world war. When the United States joined the earlier conflict in 1917, black leaders had shared a reluctance to fully embrace the call to arms of a country so often engaged in racial discrimination at home. President Wilson's mission for Americans to "make the world safe for democracy" should rightly first begin at home, many civil rights leaders reasoned. Nevertheless, after some early hand-wringing, African Americans rallied to the patriotic goal of first serving the nation and expecting basic civil rights upon the war's end.

No one better represented this calculated gamble than W. E. B. Du Bois. The brilliant champion of civil rights and editor of the NAACP's influential periodical *Crisis* had urged African Americans to join the war effort in the expectation that "out of this war will rise an American Negro with the right to vote, with the right to work, and the right to live without insult." As those black veterans carried their war wounds and pride back to a postwar America, Du Bois now urged them to "return fighting" for equality. While they had helped win the war in Europe, the black soldier soon found that white Americans dug a trench far deeper at home to maintain their long-standing white supremacy. Not only did African Americans fail to win their constitutional rights, white mobs also attacked black slums in a terrible harvest of race riots across the country in the summer of 1919. The so-called Red Summer even included the lynching of ten black soldiers in their military uniforms.

African Americans' still smoldering resentments from the previous conflict surfaced in a number of ways that certainly unsettled many white Americans. Over two years of World War II raged overseas before America's entry, and the debate escalated over whether the United States could reasonably remain neutral. As an increasing chorus of white Americans began anticipating an American entry in the days before Pearl Harbor, many black leaders voiced considerable skepticism. The renowned black newspaper *The Chicago Defender* ran a 1940 satirical article depicting a mock Nazi invasion of the United States. The incursion would be successful, it chided, due to invaluable aid from southern senators and allied white racists. Other black journalists joined the skeptical isolationist stance of this "white man's war," asking "[W]hat is there to choose between the British in Africa, and the rule of the

Germans in Africa?" Another celebrated the possibility that whites might "mow one another down" for a change rather than "quietly murder hundreds of thousands of Africans, East Indians, and Chinese." *Crisis*, the journal of the NAACP, regretted the "brutality, blood and death among the peoples of Europe just as we were sorry for China and Ethiopia. But the hysterical cries of the preachers of democracy for Europe leave us cold. We want democracy in Alabama and Arkansas, in Mississippi and Michigan, in the District of Columbia—*in the Senate of the United States*."

While such African American criticism softened after Pearl Harbor, these rumblings in the African American community deeply concerned those in the halls of government. Secretary of War Henry L. Stimson saw domestic racial tensions as "explosive" and harbored private concerns in his diary that African Americans' continuing calls for equality were part of a broader conspiracy backed by Japanese and communist elements. Stimson, in fact, feared that "a good many" black leaders received bribes during the war from the Japanese ambassador to Mexico as part of a "systematic campaign" to induce African American calls for racial change. Even the white moderate social scientist Gunnar Myrdal, while underscoring African Americans' wartime loyalty, took note of some disquieting trends in his 1944 landmark racial study, *An American Dilemma*. A small number of blacks, he asserted, found "vicarious satisfaction in imagining a Japanese (or German) invasion of the Southern states." More troubling still was the possibility of unresolved African American grievances after the war, he wrote, which could lead to divided loyalties "if later a new war were to be fought more definitely along color lines."

The newly formed Congress of Racial Equality used the leverage of wartime propaganda in a campaign of demonstrations against segregated accommodations, carrying picketing placards—for example, in Washington, D.C., in 1944 a placard read, "Are you for Hitler's Way or the American Way?" The *Pittsburgh Courier* (which promoted the "Double V" campaign for victory abroad against the Axis Powers and at home against white supremacy) portrayed the war as an excellent "opportunity . . . to persuade, embarrass, compel and shame our government and our nation . . . into a more enlightened attitude" on the racial question.

Reluctant or not, Robinson reported for his draft call in early April 1942, and was shipped for basic training to Fort Riley, Kansas. He promptly applied for Officer Candidate School. He and his black colleagues passed the tests for qualification but received no word for months, as Robinson began to understand that Jim Crow's hand was at work—not surprising given that the

Secretary of War Stimson himself maintained that "leadership is not embedded in the Negro race." Army Chief of Staff George Marshall had already resolved that desegregating the army would demolish wartime morale by unnecessarily disturbing the national mores "established by the American people through custom and habit." Robinson was relegated to the stables to look after the horses.

White supremacy extended into every aspect of a soldier's life, as the All-American stable hand was barred from the base's baseball team as well. A defiant Robinson refused a senior officer's request that he join the football team instead (in a sport where the customs of segregation were less ingrained). He had first agreed to play, until he was informed that he must sit whenever the opponent declined to play an integrated team. The angry white colonel, who was eager to strengthen the team since his son was a member, threatened to order Robinson, but Robinson remained recalcitrant. The two denials did not stop the remarkably multifaceted athletic talent entirely during his military service, as he became the U.S. Army's table tennis champion during the war.

While languishing in the limitations of a Jim Crow army, an increasingly disaffected Robinson found some unexpected good fortune. A newly arriving recruit caused a considerable stir at Fort Riley—especially among African Americans in uniform: champion boxer Joe Louis. Unquestionably, blacks recognized Louis as a heroic figure who had carried the burden of all his brethren. It was a yoke young Robinson would come to understand a decade hence, but, for now, Robinson was the chin-dropping admirer of the "Brown Bomber"—a conqueror who had physically dominated whites in an era where doing so outside a ring might get you killed. It was said that African Americans without a radio needn't leave their homes to listen to a Louis match. Since all blacks who could huddle around a radio console had the events blaring, one simply sat on the stoop or fire escape to soak up the broadcasts in any black neighborhood in the country.

Managers who assiduously sought to avoid any association with Louis's predecessor black champion, Jack Johnson, closely guided Louis's fighting career. Johnson, who held the heavyweight title from 1908 to 1912, had openly courted controversy through his ostentatious lifestyle, defiant attitude toward whites, and liaisons with white women. While all these practices brought deep white resentments, the latter in particular aroused tremendous consternation. Johnson's patent refusal to court white approval would cast a lengthy shadow over black athletes for decades to come. The gendered tradition of viewing athletic prowess as an important marker of manhood made this particularly unnerving to white audiences. (As a sign of how far Johnson would go to defy whites' needs to be reassured about their racialized insecurities, Johnson wrapped his penis during sparring matches to make it appear very much the oversized organ of racial mythology.)

If Louis was to have any chance at a title bout, he would need to steer considerably clear of reminding whites of the flamboyant Johnson. With that in mind, his black manager, John Roxborough, devised a set of "commandments" to be followed closely by the "Brown Bomber." They included: never be photographed with a white woman, never "gloat over a fallen opponent" (which was part of a general directive that he should remain modest, humble, and soft-spoken at all times), and, above all, "live and fight clean." His agents carefully choreographed his press coverage, showing Louis being tutored two hours a day and receiving a Bible from his mother before a big fight. While racially charged depictions of Louis continued to appear in the press throughout his career, his handlers' efforts clearly paid off in plaudits like the *New York Herald Tribune*'s: "Joe Louis is as different a character from Jack Johnson as [the widely beloved Yankee first baseman] Lou Gehrig is from Al Capone. . . . He is a God-fearing, Bible-reading, clean-living young man, to be admired, regardless of creed, race, or color. He is neither a show-off, nor a dummy. Modest, quiet, unassuming in his manner, he goes about his business, doing the best job he can every time he climbs into a ring." Louis's impression as an unthreatening black male became a critical part of his ability to win further financial opportunities. It was a lesson not lost on Robinson and his superiors in the years to come. As Robinson himself said years later, "If it wasn't for Joe Louis, the color line in baseball would not have been broken for another ten years."

It was Louis's renowned 1938 rematch against German Max Schmeling, however, that earned, finally, broader support of a reluctant white public. Schmeling's 1936 surprise defeat of the mighty Louis had helped confirm an admiring Adolph Hitler's theories of Aryan superiority. Louis's victory two years hence wiped the slate clean again, and allowed Americans an early victory against the increasingly despised racist German dictator that they would soon face on European battlefields. When the war broke out, Louis joined the military in a highly publicized fashion, orchestrated both by his handlers and a U.S. Army eager to use the pugilist to court black favor for the war effort. Louis toured military bases shaking recruits' hands and engaging in sparring exhibitions, and even fought several benefit title matches for military charities.

Figure 2.1.   Given African American resentment over the harsh treatment accorded black veterans following the previous world war, the U.S. government worried about black popular support for World War II. The U.S. military thus enlisted popular boxer Joe Louis to generate African American support in promotional posters and public appearances. *Source*: Library of Congress, http://www.loc.gov/item/201564580

Now that Louis was assigned to Fort Riley, he was swamped by his adoring fellow recruits, including the young Robinson, with whom he began a lifelong friendship. Louis, in fact, had heard of Robinson's athletic prowess, and the two shared some afternoon rounds of golf, where Robinson also shared some grievances about black soldiers' conditions on the base. Louis passed these stories up to an old friend now serving in the Pentagon: Truman Gibson, then an assistant to William Hastie, African American aide to the Secretary of War. Gibson flew to Fort Riley himself and met with Robinson and other black soldiers to study these conditions. Days later, Robinson and several other blacks finally received swift invitations to Officer Candidate School (OCS). As they arrived, those black servicemen took part in an extraordinary experiment: the first time the U.S. Army allowed an integrated environment at OCS in the midst of a still rigidly segregated military.

Gibson recounts a subsequent intervention by Louis during Robinson's stint in OCS. Hearing a white captain call a soldier "a stupid black nigger son of bitch," an enraged Robinson demanded an apology. "That goes for you, too, nigger," the captain responded. Robinson's "explosive temper" now took flight with a punch that took out the white officer's front teeth. The famed boxer, aware that his new friend Robinson faced a potential court martial for his own pugilism, "immediately called" Gibson. During a later special meeting with the commanding officer, Gibson and Louis pleaded for leniency. According to Gibson, only Louis's offering of several gifts saved Robinson. The prizefighter later proudly purchased new uniforms for the new black officer graduates. Robinson never forgot Louis, his assistance, nor his willingness to fight in and out of the ring. Years later, Robinson would say, "Joe Louis has done a great thing for our race. . . . I am going in [to Major League baseball] with a much greater advantage than Joe had . . . and I will try to carry on."

Now a second lieutenant, Robinson made full use of his assignment as morale officer to push the boundaries of a segregated army. One notable incident began over the paucity of "Negro" seating arrangements at the post exchange. African American troops often went wanting for chairs while the "white" seats were empty. After numerous complaints by his men, Robinson took the matter up with an unsympathetic provost marshal, Major Hafner, who mistook the lieutenant's phone voice for a white man (no doubt due to the simple fact that he was an officer—a rarity for a soldier of color).

The major cautioned Robinson that desegregating the exchange "would become a real problem and might adversely affect the morale of our white troops." As the conversation grew increasingly heated, the exasperated major sought to ground his concerns with a simple question: "Lieutenant, let me put it to you this way. How would you like to have your wife sitting next to a nigger?" An already irritated Robinson exploded with what he recalled was "pure rage." Surprised to discover that he was speaking to a lieutenant on the wrong side of the color line, Hafner could only say that he most assuredly didn't "want my wife sitting close to any colored guy." By now, Robinson was "shouting at the top of my voice. Every typewriter in headquarters stopped. The clerks were frozen in disbelief at the way I ripped into the major." Having gone this far, the USC track star now ran full tilt across the line of acceptable racial mores by posing a taboo question to Hafner: "How the hell do you know that your wife hasn't already been close to one?" That produced a dial tone in Robinson's ear.

Robinson's uncompromising stand was not entirely fruitless. While the exchange remained segregated, a few additional seats did open there for black personnel. "I ought to get at least a battle star if I can capture three stools from the enemy at the post exchange," he lamented over the major battle still facing blacks in uniform. Having won this rather muted concession from Fort Riley brass, Lt. Robinson carried his determination to improve racial matters further south to an even less hospitable civil rights climate: Fort Hood, Texas.

Aptly named after Confederate Civil War general John Bell Hood, the installation had a notorious reputation among African American soldiers. As one of Robinson's fellow black officers recalls, blacks' treatment at Fort Hood made other military bases (hardly known as racially progressive) seem comparatively "ultraliberal. . . . Camp Hood was frightening. . . . Segregation there was so complete I even saw outhouses marked White, Colored, and Mexican." A host of segregated on-base accommodations were compounded by an even more hostile local civilian population greeting black servicemen on leave.

The inevitable collision of the determined young second lieutenant and his new Jim Crow surroundings arrived in July 1944 in a setting all too familiar with a famous launching pad for the civil rights movement a decade later: a bus. Long before Rosa Parks took her fateful ride, southern buses had become a tangible and degrading reminder of white supremacy. For black soldiers who might soon die for their country, that was doubly so. As such, incidents on buses near and around southern military bases had begun to mount. Just a few weeks prior to Robinson's ride, an enraged bus driver in Durham, North Carolina, had shot a black passenger dead for refusing to move to the rear. A jury subsequently acquitted the shooter. But Robinson was emboldened by the action of his idol, Joe Louis, a few months earlier. On a military public relations tour, Louis and fellow black boxer, Sugar Ray Robinson, had refused to move to colored seating at Alabama's Camp Sibert bus depot. "We ain't moving," Louis had told the MP simply. Then escorted to an angry provost marshal, Louis threatened to "call Washington." The white officer relented, but the incident aroused embarrassing newspaper ink and resulted in a new army order for desegregated buses.

Lt. Robinson was well aware of these recent directives when he stepped onto Milton Renegar's bus on July 6, 1944. Robinson had observed segregation on city buses at his off-base medical exam, but now that he arrived on base, he took a seat halfway down the aisle next to Virginia Jones, the wife of a fellow black officer. Renegar had kept close tabs on Robinson and the light-skinned Mrs. Jones in his rearview mirror, and, according to Robinson, surely "saw what he thought was a white woman talking with a black second lieutenant." If accurate, this perceived violation of one of the most sacred taboos of southern white supremacy would be important context for what happened next. After five blocks, Renegar halted the bus and angrily insisted Robinson move to the rear "where colored people belong," since he "had a load of [white] ladies to pick up and . . . was sure they wouldn't want to ride mixed up [desegregated] like that." When Robinson stood his ground, Renegar threatened that continued refusal "would cause [Robinson] plenty of trouble." A defiant Robinson replied "hotly that I couldn't care less about his causing me trouble. I'd been in trouble all my life, but I knew what my rights were."

By the time the bus arrived at the last stop, the driver stormed off to his dispatcher to report the "incident." Clearly violating white southern social mores, Robinson had upset not just the driver. An unhinged white saleswoman who had served Robinson at the post exchange had had her fill, and loudly indicated to white officials that she was eager to testify against the insolent black lieutenant. As she put it later, "I asked the bus driver if he was going to report him, and I told him that if he didn't report the colored lieutenant that I was going to report him to the MPs. I had to wait on them during the day, but I didn't have to sit with them on the bus." As a white crowd began to gather, the dispatcher and two other drivers confronted Robinson, who turned on them to "stop f***ing with me," punctuated with his finger stabbing toward the white faces as MPs arrived. Robinson voluntarily went with them, partly because they called him "sir," and partly because he believed he had nothing to fear from actions that were "well within my rights."

Just as the matters might have calmed down with Robinson safely confined to the MP jeep, Private Mucklerath stirred Robinson's considerable anger again by asking the MPs whether they had "that nigger lieutenant" in the vehicle. Robinson addressed the white private as a "son of a bitch" who had best refrain from using that word. "I'm an officer and God damn you, you better address me as one." To underscore the point, Robinson assured Mucklerath that he would "break him in two" if he ever used the word again. Mucklerath was shaken enough by the way Robinson delivered the line that he later requested that all those present record it in their statements.

At the Military Police station, Captain Gerald Bear had already heard the white bus driver's account. Bear next chose to interview the white private, telling Lt. Robinson he must wait outside. Mucklerath, in fact, had simply walked into Bear's office against a standing order that all would wait until called. When Robinson was reprimanded for trying to do the same, Robinson challenged Bear for apparently privileging the white testimony. Bear bristled and commanded Robinson again to stand clear. When Robinson was finally admitted, the captain demanded to know why the lieutenant wanted to "start a race riot." (Wartime race riots were no idle concern, as such incidents produced thirty-four dead in Detroit and six in Harlem in the previous year. Even more concerning to a military official would have been the racial conflagrations on several military bases. At Mississippi's Camp Van Dorn, African American soldiers raided a stockade and battled local authorities. In Georgia, black troops seized submachine guns from Camp Stewart's arsenal, killing a military policeman.)

Captain Bear's civilian secretary then took over the interrogation herself: Why would he sit intentionally "where no colored people are supposed to sit" in a deliberate effort "to start some trouble"? When Robinson protested having to answer to a civilian assistant, Bear labeled the lieutenant as "uppity." The secretary now persisted, "Lieutenant, did you not deliberately pick that seat although there were others in the back?" When Robinson replied that clearly he wouldn't have sat down in that seat unless he did so "deliberately," she had had enough of the black officer, contending, "I don't have to take that sassy kind of talk from you."

Captain Bear took great offense and "began to rave," said Robinson, defending "traditional southern chivalry for wounded white womanhood." Robinson turned the tables by asking Bear where he was from, which the captain took as an assessment of his potential southern racist background. Bear offered evidence of his racial enlightenment: "that back home he owned a laundry, and that he employed a number of blacks—and all the rest of that stuff that bigots talk when confronted with the charge of being bigots," recounted Robinson. Undergirding Robinson's belief that he "was up against one of those white supremacy characters," Bear "did not seem to recognize me as an officer at all; but I did consider myself an officer and felt that I should be addressed as one." Refusing to play his assigned role in this all-too-familiar racial drama, Robinson well knew that "[e]verything would have been all right if I had been a 'yassuh boss' type." The white captain would come to claim that Robinson engaged in a host of insubordinate actions that evening, including refusal to obey an order to remain seated in the waiting area and "acting in an insolent, impertinent and rude manner." The latter claim allegedly included "contemptuously bowing" and "several sloppy salutes."

When the statements were finally concluded, a clearly unsettled Bear was determined to make the black lieutenant pay. When Bear brought court martial papers to Colonel R. L. Bates, Robinson's white superior, Bates refused to sign them. Robinson had long ago "come to regard [Bates] as a wonderful officer who understood the special problems faced by Negro troops, and who insisted upon fair treatment of all the people under his command." The feeling was apparently mutual as the 761st Tank Battalion commander had already singled Robinson out for special commendation, and eagerly testified on Robinson's behalf in the coming court martial. Hellbent that the "uppity" black lieutenant's behavior would not stand, Bear now successfully insisted that Robinson be transferred to another battalion with a more compliant white commander—who promptly agreed to Robinson's court martial.

With the black lieutenant's charges newly signed, word began to spread among Camp Hood's African American servicemen that "here was another case," Robinson recalled, "in which a Negro soldier was about to be offered up on the altar of segregation." Indeed, the NAACP had already received word that "this incident is only one of many which have seen Negro officers and enlisted men intimidated and mistreated in Camp Hood." A disturbed group of black Camp Hood officers wrote to the NAACP, and alerted two of the most renowned black newspapers, The Chicago Defender and the Pittsburgh Courier. The Pittsburgh Courier, in particular, was then "one of the country's most powerful weeklies," Robinson recounted, and shone "important publicity" on his plight.

Robinson also began writing—to Truman Gibson and then to the NAACP, asking for "a civilian lawyer to handle my case because I know he will be able to force the truth with a little technique" since the whites involved "had got together . . . to frame me" with "a pretty good bunch of lies." (The NAACP, inundated with requests from numerous black soldiers, indicated it would be unable to help.) Robinson recognized that the military would be "sensitive to this kind of spotlight" and could see that "if I was unfairly treated, it would not be a secret." There is in fact evidence that the escalating attention began to cause Camp Hood military brass considerable concern. As XXIII Corps Chief of Staff Walter Buie put it to a fellow colonel: "This is a very serious case, and it is full of dynamite. It requires very delicate handling . . . and I am afraid that any officer in charge of troops at this Post might be prejudiced." In light of this mounting pressure, the more serious charges would be dropped.

As the court date approached, even finding an attorney to represent the defiant Robinson presented a dilemma. The military appointed a thirty-two-year-old white southerner who "had the decency to admit" to the black defendant that he couldn't "do a fair job of defending" him. It wasn't that he harbored "deep prejudices against Negroes," he confided to his potential client. "It's just that, having grown up in a segregated society, I haven't developed arguments against segregation that I feel I would need as a background to defend you adequately." An attorney from Michigan took his place, who, in Robinson's own estimation, "did a great job."

The court martial of Lieutenant Jack R. Robinson took place on August 2, 1944. The lieutenant had the weight of evidence on his side, and his attorney had little trouble pointing out that the prosecutorial witnesses appeared to provide rehearsed testimony that conflicted with their original statements. Furthermore, much of the behavior that Captain Bear had considered inappropriate and insubordinate might have been problematic if Robinson had been under an "at attention" command, but had actually taken place while the defendant had been ordered "at ease." This left the obvious assumption that Bear had subjectively taken offense at the black lieutenant's demeanor not because of military regulations, but because of southern racial custom. Robinson's attorney summed up the case as "simply a situation in which a few individuals sought to vent their bigotry on a Negro they considered 'uppity' because he had the audacity to seek to exercise rights that belonged to him as an American and as a soldier." The court martial board included one officer who was "obviously a southerner," but he was offset by an alumnus of UCLA and an African American captain. It found him not guilty by a two-thirds margin.

During the court martial, Robinson's unit had finally received the long-sought call for overseas action in Europe. Robinson's 761st Battalion distinguished itself as the first black armored unit in combat, and participated in the liberation of the Buchenwald concentration camp. But these would not be distinctions earned by Lieutenant Robinson. His court martial had caused him to miss the boat, and Robinson now found himself "pretty much fed up with the service." His battle, of course, was not to be in occupied Europe.

CHAPTER THREE

The World of Black Baseball

In 1872, Bud Fowler put on a glove for a New Castle, Pennsylvania, team and became the first paid black professional baseball player. Bouncing around a number of teams in the 1870s and 1880s, Fowler was regarded as one of the game's best second basemen. Not without white detractors, Fowler began wearing wooden shin guards to protect himself from racist players' frequent intentional sliding into his legs. By 1885, he found himself without a team home. "The poor fellow's skin is against him," lamented the national magazine *Sporting Life*. Still, meager progress was made to allow some twenty African American players to sign into white organized baseball by 1887. Rising white players' complaints, though, forced the clubs to begin dropping their darker teammates from the squads. Even the light-skinned black catcher Richard Johnson was exposed by a white Syracuse team as living under an assumed name and white racial identity in order to play. As Jim Crow hardened in American society, so it did in baseball. The close of the nineteenth century brought the sunset of black players' participation in white professional leagues.

The alternative rise of black baseball coincided with that of the segregation system. Many African Americans had entered the postbellum era with high hopes of equality and advancement only to see those dreams slowly vanish in the 1880s and 1890s. The 1896 *Plessy v. Ferguson* Supreme Court ruling, which legally permitted Jim Crow, was the last nail in that coffin. Some blacks now turned toward their only alternative—nurturing their own segregated institutions. The talented African American players, with nowhere else to ply their trade, began forming teams of their own. But these new black clubs, hampered by the white establishment's refusal to admit them into regular league play, would instead seek out games on an ad hoc basis with white teams. Traveling long distances at times in search of a pay-check, this evolved into the wide practice of "barnstorming"—which consisted of clubs engaging in exhibition tours across the country or even into Latin America.

The fact that African American baseball, like African Americans in general, always had to battle economic limitations led to a number of distinctive realities for blacks in the sport. The wider use of barnstorming by black clubs represented one expression of that as more money was made than in traditional Negro League play. This held some black teams hostage to extended travel and reshuffled league game schedules whenever a more lucrative exhibition opportunity appeared. On Sunday, most Negro leaguers played three games to accommodate the greater crowds available on what might be the only off day for many of their African American working-class fans. The third, or "twilight," game would be positioned to begin following the end-of-the-day shift, as some blacks got no days off at all.

Although a number of teams (including white clubs) also occasionally practiced strange gimmicks to attract crowds, a few black clubs became particularly noted for the phenomenon. The Zulu Cannibal Giants, for example, showcased their team in grass skirts and war paint and engaged in comedic shows between games, which included black players fighting with spears. The Ethiopian Clowns, seen by some to be more of a comedy act than a professional baseball team, used face painting and player pseudonyms such as "Wahoo" and "Tarzan" to draw considerable crowds across the 1930s Midwest. The renowned black sportswriter Wendell Smith, taking obvious offense to the way such clubs cemented racial stereotypes, lamented the Clowns' performances as essentially "minstrel shows."

The first truly sustained black baseball league (eight teams in all) began in 1920: the Negro National League. Despite strong attendance during the decade that followed, the onset of the Great Depression sunk the League, as it did so many other economic enterprises. Black baseball persisted, but only as independent, traveling teams. It was not until 1933 that an organized league of black clubs was once again established. The resurrected Negro National League, based on the eastern seaboard, was soon joined in 1937 by the Negro American League, based in the Midwest and South.

Though Rube Foster (the African American owner of the renowned Chicago American Giants) began the 1920 National Negro League determined to "keep Colored baseball from the control of whites," Negro League owners dreamed of a day when their black clubs might be incorporated into the Major Leagues. Aware that full American social integration might be a long way off, Foster and others saw blending full Negro League clubs into the white Majors (as opposed to integrating simply individual African American players) as a much more reachable horizon.

While black players continued to build their separate world of the Negro Leagues, white teams remained determined to block access for their African American counterparts. White owners' excuses were both myriad and meager. Roughly one-third of Major Leaguers were southern, causing manager worries that an integrated team might disrupt coveted team chemistry. Racist attitudes were certainly tolerated, if not welcomed. Such 1920s greats Gabby Street, Tris Speaker, and Rogers Hornsby even bragged of Ku Klux Klan membership. And in one notable moment, 1938 New York Yankee Jake Powell revealed to radio listeners his off-season pastime as an unofficial "cop" who took "pleasure in beating up niggers and then throwing them in jail." Major League teams often took their spring training to southern climes (deemed necessary for the South's more reliable warm training weather), where blacks and whites were legally barred from sharing a field. And at least equally important, there was little economic pressure to challenge such concerns, since only one-quarter of African Americans lived above the Mason Dixon to attend potential integrated big league games. Doing the right thing by black players was seen to lack financial rewards.

On close examination, these long-used defenses for segregating America's game melt away. There may have indeed been some white southerners who would have refused to take an integrated field, but there were already some corners of barnstorming exhibitions featuring problem-free white and black competition. The coveted fame and fortune of Major League baseball (and significantly less player power in the midcentury baseball world than today) virtually ensured low numbers of white player defections if the teams had desegregated. The Brooklyn Dodgers' 1947 experiment—on a team with a field manager and prominent players hailing from Dixie—bears that out. A committed organizational front office to the enterprise—not easy to come by in sports or anywhere in 1940s America—was an essential component of this success, however. As to the difficulties of teams confronting Jim Crow in spring training, white clubs could simply go to Cuba or Latin America to find an amenable alternative. The Brooklyn Dodgers did just that when Robinson joined the team. If enough white teams had desegregated and chosen this option, one suspects that southern towns' Jim Crow commitment would have withered over the significant lost money and tourism associated with spring training.

Despite the long history of racial separation, World War II led to a grow-ing number of factors that would change America's game. The military draft's depletion of white teams' rosters during the early to mid-1940s created a window of opportunity for racial change in America's game. White owners, still fearful of crossing the color line, faced increased pressure from a small but persistent group of sports journalists, led by Wendell Smith of the renowned black newspaper the *Pittsburgh Courier*. Smith's determination for integrating baseball began in his belly as a baseball player himself, as he found his way unfairly blocked by discrimination in the early to mid-1930s. Giving in to the era's racial realities, he found his way to sports journalism instead, where he earned wide respect as one of the nation's best—of any color. Smith would later play his own important role in the entry of one Jackie Robinson. For now, though, Smith was joined not only by other black sportswriters but also by a rising number of white columnists in pressuring baseball to drop their racial restrictions.

Amid the mounting northern public pressure and the reality of the dwin-dling wartime availability of white talent, Jackie Robinson and Negro League pitcher Nate Moreland attained a tryout with the Chicago White Sox in 1942 upon their own request. Despite their obvious positive impression and Sox manager Jimmy Dykes's conclusion that Robinson was "worth $50,000 of anybody's money," the two black athletes left without an offer. (Robinson actually had suffered from a charley horse during the exhibition, leading Dykes to marvel, "I'd hate to see him on two good legs. . . . He stole every-thing but my infielders' gloves.") A similar fate awaited Buck Leonard (the so-called black Lou Gehrig) and Josh Gibson, who met with Washington Senators' Clark Griffith in 1943. While Griffith never followed up on the meeting, he had presciently warned the two athletes that day, "If we get you boys, we're going to get the best ones. It's going to break up your league." Undeterred, Leonard assured that "if that's gonna be better for the players, then it's all right by me." (Leonard never got that chance.) That same year, the Pittsburgh Pirates arranged for a tryout with two other black players, catcher Roy Campanella and pitcher Dave Barnhill, but pulled the plug before the date arrived. Two California clubs also announced tryouts for black players that year that never surfaced.

That same public pressure won Broadway great Paul Robeson a place on the baseball owners' winter meetings agenda in December 1943. Robeson, denied his own opportunity in white professional athletics in 1936, was now at the peak of his impressive career. The black thespian lettered twelve times for Rutgers University athletics, graduated Phi Beta Kappa, attained a law degree, and commanded a legendary voice that earned him the famous title role in the current Broadway production of *Othello*. Before Robeson took the room, however, Landis insisted privately to the owners, "Don't interrupt Robeson. Let's not get into any discussion with him." Robeson spoke for fifteen minutes, invited questions and comments that—true to Landis's enforced discipline—were not forthcoming, and then the owners' meeting continued undeterred and unmolested. Robeson's leftist leanings (including living in the Soviet Union in the late 1930s), no doubt, also weighed on the already unreceptive audience.

Some of the nation's journalists were not so compliant with Landis's informal gag order. The *Pittsburgh Courier*'s Wendell Smith called Landis for comment. "Each club is entirely free to employ Negro players to any extent it pleases," Landis replied disingenuously, "and the matter is solely for each club's decision without any restriction whatsoever." Nat Low of the communist *Daily Worker* did create a small firestorm by quoting Brooklyn Dodgers manager Leo Durocher on whether African Americans were talented enough for white ball clubs. "Hell, I've seen a million good ones," Durocher insisted. (Durocher, like many white former players, had a history battling very talented black teams during winter exhibitions. His white all-star teams, beginning in 1932, lost to talented black barnstormers.) When Low's story hit print, Landis hit the ceiling, and had Durocher flown immediately to his Chicago office for a closed-door lambasting. The story then died along with Durocher's pride.

Hence, the budding athlete Robinson was just as limited in employment options as was virtually any young, ambitious, black male of the postwar era. A conversation with a fellow soldier during the war did spawn his next career move. That colleague, who had first worn a Negro League Kansas City Monarchs uniform before he donned the U.S. military's, recounted to Robinson his happy memories with the club and the $400 per month that sealed those rosy recollections. When the Monarchs responded positively to Robinson's written inquiries, he began his professional baseball career by reporting to their training camp in April 1945.

The Monarchs had been one of the most respected Negro League clubs for some time. They won four Negro League pennants in the 1920s and another seven between 1937 and 1950—more than any other club. They would come to send more players into the white Majors and the Baseball Hall of Fame than any other black organization. As player Buck O'Neil recalled, the reason that the Monarchs had "such good ball clubs was like the [Major League New York] Yankees. If you were a player and a scout came

Figure 3.1. Robinson, as a member of the renowned Negro Leagues club, the Kansas City Monarchs, 1945. *Source*: Library of Congress, http://www.loc.gov/pictures/item/97518994/

to your door from the Yankees and one came from another team, your eyes would light up for the Yankees. Same with the Monarchs. Everybody wanted to come and play with the Kansas City Monarchs." Another player recalled an intelligent professionalism that set the Monarchs apart not only from Negro League ball but from the white Major Leagues as well. While other teams might discuss hitting and pitching strategies against the day's opponent prior to the contest, the Monarchs singularly dissected the games after their conclusion as well. Monarch pitcher Connie Johnson, who later signed with the Major Leagues' Chicago White Sox, recalled that "one thing we did here . . . that the Majors never did. They never did talk about the game. The games's over, that's it. Whether you win or lose, [the Monarchs] were talking about the game—what happened, what we could have did, what we didn't do" into the wee hours.

The Monarchs' reputation had indeed earned them an impressive roster. In recent years they had attracted Othello Renfroe, Willard Brown, Hank Thompson, Hilton Smith, and Bullet Joe Rogan. No figure on its current roster was more notable than legendary pitcher Satchel Paige. Renowned for his blistering fastball, and—as he grew older—a mystifying array of pitches, Paige was famous for his supreme self-confidence and colorful showboating. He would sometimes promise to strike out the first nine batters—and meet the pledge—call his outfielders into the infield to pitch without their defensive support, or announce his unhittable pitch in advance to further frustrate bewildered batters. By the early 1930s, a young player could make a name for himself simply by hitting a Paige pitch. Several years of famous barnstorming showdowns left a profound impression on Major League pitching legend Dizzy Dean. While many of his white peers would cite the white Hall of Famer as the greatest pitcher they ever faced, Dean—hardly noted for his racial progressivism—had another in mind for that title in his 1938 newspaper column: "I know whose the best pitcher I ever see and it's old Satchel Paige. . . . [O]ld Diz is pretty fast back in 1933 and 1934, and you know my fast ball looks like a change of pace alongside that little pistol bullet old Satchel shoots up to the plate. . . . It's too bad those colored boys don't play in the big leagues, because they sure got some great players."

Also telling was an encounter in 1936 between Paige and the iconic Joe DiMaggio. Still a twenty-one-year-old Minor Leaguer, the New York Yankees wanted to confirm what they might have in the young white player. They did so by calling north Satchel Paige to match him. When DiMaggio managed a slim single in four at-bats against Paige, a delighted Yankee scout saw proof that DiMaggio was destined for glory, wiring superiors, "DIMAGGIO ALL

WE HOPED HE'D BE. HIT SATCH ONE FOR FOUR." The fact that white Major League executives chose the Negro Leaguer as the best test of a white player's mettle, and saw one for four as extraordinary success, spoke volumes about the hypocrisy of dividing baseball on the color line under claims of black inferiority. Years later, DiMaggio joined Dean and others in counting Paige as the greatest pitcher he ever encountered, claiming his curveball was "like a wiggle in a cyclone" and his lightning fastball left the receiving catcher with "nothing but ashes."

Sequestered to shadow leagues in segregated America, African American players had to endure further limitations. Negro League players and officials were subject to constant obstacles and frustrations, as blacks surely were in the broader society. Negro League players rarely took a field controlled by their owners. It was standard for the teams to rent arenas from white teams—producing one more reason for white owners' opposition to integrating the game. The separate black teams played in stadiums when the white team was absent, thus providing an important source of additional income to white clubs. These rental arrangements also served as an unpleasant reminder of blacks' subservience. African American athletes were routinely denied access to the parks' locker rooms and showers. Major League clubs also bumped Negro club dates when a more lucrative rental presented itself (a boxing match, for example), which could play havoc with Negro League scheduling.

The financially strapped black teams often lacked the full training in baseball fundamentals that their white counterparts enjoyed. Denied the Major Leagues' economic resources, they had little time to engage in extended professional training beyond paid games. While this could result in a lack of playing polish, it also meant the black game was more improvisational, and, to many observers, more interesting and innovative. By the 1920s, white baseball had been overshadowed by Babe Ruth and the love of the home run. White players were thus often educated to be more conservative, getting on base and awaiting their power-hitting teammate who might knock them in with a single blast.

While the Negro Leagues did boast prodigious power hitters, they were also far more inclined to use speed, base stealing, and "tricky baseball." The latter involved a variety of risky and sometimes unorthodox tactics. As Negro League great Newt Allen recalled, "[I]n boxing there's two rules, Queensbury [the staid, official, gentlemanly standard] and the one called 'coonsbury.' We played the coonsbury rules. That's just any way you think you can win, any kind of play you think you can get by with." For pitching legend Satchel

Paige, the more conservative brand of white baseball was much less challeng-ing. He credited his longevity beyond age forty in the Major Leagues with white players' overreliance on the homer. "That was like cool water to me," claimed the forty-two-year-old Major Leaguer. A judicious black player not given a ball to send beyond the fences could instead drive a single and wreak havoc with speed and base stealing. Cool Papa Bell was the Negro League artist at the latter. Satchel Paige maintained that the speedy Bell "could flip the switch and get into bed before the room went dark." Jackie Robinson, of course, left the Negro Leagues and then, not surprisingly, made perhaps his biggest splash in the Majors with his speed and base-running savvy.

Black pitchers were also known to commonly alter the ball to produce unpredictable results. Catcher Roy Campanella (destined to break in to the Major League Brooklyn team one year after Robinson, and earn a spot in the Major League Hall of Fame) remembers that "[a]nything went in the Negro National League. Spitballs, shine balls, emery balls; pitchers used any and all of them. They nicked and moistened and treated the ball to make it flutter and spin and break. One simple additional reason for the tolerance of altered balls could sometimes be the limited number of new replacement balls. The greater resourced white Major Leagues could stock enough balls to take the place of a scuffed one; the Negro Leagues might just throw it back into play.

Nevertheless, black baseball became one of the largest Jim Crow–era com-mercial enterprises in the African American community. Baseball was also the only sport that offered an African American a livable wage—with the rare exception of boxer Joe Louis. One factor that ensured its success was the continuing practice of barnstorming. From February to April, Negro League teams began a short season of barnstorming, usually across the South, which gave blacks below the Mason Dixon an important taste of the famous brand of black baseball played by these mostly northern black teams. Negro Leagu-ers would play each other, a team from a historically African American col-lege, or simply a local team.

For many rural African Americans, the arrival of a barnstorming black team was a most welcome respite from the drudgery of both grinding discrim-ination and the still-common malaise of everyday country life. Many of those small communities supported local semipro teams, and the appearance of a famed Negro League or black all-star team created what one historian called a "holiday atmosphere," including outdoor dinners with players on Main Street following the game.

After working their way North through their flurry of popular southern exhibitions during the two months of barnstorming, the mass celebration of

Negro League season opening day arrived in their home cities. The Negro League teams often became central rallying and unifying points for those local black communities—especially on the Sunday games when the mostly working-class fans could get to the park. From opening-day public player banquets to ballpark beauty contests and parades, black baseball provided an important galvanizing influence on the local African American community. Black businesses, understanding this, widely participated as sponsors of events and advertisers of games. Their store windows were often littered with players' promotions of products. Even white-owned enterprises relying on black dollars contributed some of that profit back to black baseball to earn customer loyalty.

Sunday games attracted not only sports fans but also anyone who wanted to see and be seen in the black community. That was especially true on opening day, where the game capped a daylong celebration. Local African Americans, claimed *The Chicago Defender* in 1923, poured out in droves, "like a lot of bees hidden away all winter." Women in their finery, regional notables, and black entertainment stars were all on display. Whenever jazz great Count Basie found himself in Kansas City on a Sunday, he went to the Monarchs' game, "because that's where everyone else was going on a Sunday afternoon." The list of notables present would certainly include politicians (black and white alike), who quickly learned that the ballpark was the best way to show support for and win allegiance from the gathered black community. Mayors in the 1930s regularly appeared at big-city black ballparks on opening day. Some Negro Leagues strikingly outdrew crowds for the competing local white teams. In short, Negro baseball had become the fastest-growing sector of the black economy by World War II.

Some of the Negro League owners turned their spotlights into more explicit attacks on racial problems. Indianapolis ABCs' owner Olivia Taylor also ran the city's NAACP chapter. Effa Manley, vocal and visible owner of the Newark Eagles, was not only a state NAACP official, she used games to raise funds for a variety of civil rights issues as well—most notably for the "Stop Lynching" campaign, where usherettes circulated the crowd gathering money for the cause.

Despite its notable popularity in the African American community, Robinson never found himself a satisfying home in the world of black baseball. He brought the same passion and impatience for change to Negro League ball that had caused him to chafe repeatedly against other obstacles in his life. His apprehension had begun years earlier during an encounter with a barnstorming black team while attending college as an impressionable eighteen-year-old. Agreeing to fill in for a missing player, the team later stiffed the hard-playing Robinson on his $20 payday. Disturbed by the lack of professionalism, "I decided then and there that Negro baseball was not for me," he wrote in 1955.

Many of Robinson's sour recollections of his year with black ball can be easily seen through the prism of his ultimate rise into the white leagues. With that in mind, Robinson's complaints can be understood in several lights: Robinson's defense of the Dodgers' management decision to pluck him from a Negro League club, which gave him his first chance; the simple reality that black clubs could never command the financial resources to make them a true rival for the professionalism and pay of their white counterparts; and the daily maddening discrimination that African American players encountered in their travels that black owners could do little to mute.

In an early harbinger of things to come, Robinson first took the field for the Monarchs just two days after reporting and without benefit of a single practice, since rain denied the opportunity in the intervening day. To the exacting Robinson's dismay, the Negro Leagues lacked any real "spring training," a critical period of preparation before the regular season begins in the white Major Leagues. Players also endured subpar accommodations, Robinson later recalled, from the "uncomfortable buses" to hotels "of the cheapest kind" featuring bathrooms in "such bad condition that the players are unable to use them"; or, in some cases, no hotels serving black players could be found at all. As a result, the teams found themselves too frequently playing games "half asleep." The sapped players then took the field with umpires "quite often untrained and [who] favor certain teams." Robinson recounted a game in Baltimore in which players noticed an insufficient score for the Monarchs. The discrepancy was clarified when the team was informed that the park's official scorekeeper had simply become "bored with the game and went home early." The lack of professional oversight on the field only mirrored "lax" supervision by management off of it. "On many days," Robinson chagrined, "some of the players would not get to bed at all. They were allowed to drink whenever they pleased." Negro League owners, Robinson insisted, needed "to place more emphasis on the character and morals of the men they select."

But one man's disturbing lack of professional preparation was another's admirable toughness despite the odds. Most Negro Leaguers prided themselves on a signature ability to go well beyond what more pampered white stars withstood. Since owners usually did not own their stadiums, rainouts meant a ruinous loss of money; hence, games would simply continue in the dangerous, stormy conditions. Players would be sent back to the field with otherwise sidelining injuries. To ensure teams' financial viability, Negro League officials sharply limited the number of players per team (to only fifteen, for example). That meant players not only played more frequently but also pitchers played on the field on days off from pitching—a risk of injury rarely taken by white clubs with a larger roster. Some pitchers, such as Dick Redding and Smokey Joe Williams, even earned fame for pitching both games of a doubleheader (where taking at least a few days off between single pitching starts was customary in white baseball).

Compounding mistakes and incompetence by African American league and team officials was the world of segregation outside the baselines. Finding "even passable eating places" became "almost a daily problem," given the common restrictions on serving blacks inside. "You were lucky," lamented Robinson, "if they magnanimously permitted you to carry out some greasy hamburgers in a paper bag with a container of coffee." If other veteran players made understandable if uneasy accommodation to a white supremacist system they felt frequently powerless to alter, Robinson seemed to be constantly anxious to break free of these restrictions. One teammate recalled traveling "miles and miles on the bus" as the team engaged in baseball talk and friendly chatter. By contrast, Robinson's "whole talk was 'Well you guys better get ready because pretty soon baseball's going to sign one of us.'" When Robinson encountered southern segregation at gas stations along the way, "a couple of times we had to leave without our change, he'd get so mad." All in all, Negro League baseball was, for Robinson, "a pretty miserable way to make a buck."

Added to Robinson's critique was the questionable business dealings of some Negro League owners. Gus Greenlee, the owner of the famous Pittsburgh Crawfords and the chief organizer of the second National Negro League, set the mark as head of Pittsburgh's lucrative "numbers" racket (a system whereby working-class blacks bet as little as a penny to duplicate a daily changing three-digit number—most commonly the last three numbers of the stock exchange volume—to pay off at six hundred to one odds). The popularity of the numbers trade in America's black ghettos and the participation of its racketeers in Negro League baseball said much about America in the early twentieth century. The black working class enjoyed limited financial opportunities. Whereas whites would be earning far more per capita, they would have greater investment opportunities in everything from the widening stock market of the 1920s to home mortgages and simple savings accounts. A penny or a nickel might be all most blacks had left after rent and three meals, and "the numbers" promised a moment of financial glory if the sun shone on them. The fact that African Americans in the criminal underworld—especially those involved in "the numbers" racket—became some of black America's most visible entrepreneurs highlighted the lack of other black businessmen with the available capital to invest in a large business undertaking. That raw reality was well understood by their fellow blacks who faced the same barriers, and the illegal trade "numbers kings" thus often bore little stigma in the black ghettos of urban America. The novelist Richard Wright spoke for many in black America when he recognized that the "numbers kings" "would have been steel tycoons, Wall Street brokers, auto moguls had they been white."

On the other hand, the African American community's leniency was expected to be returned. The accumulated capital held by these numbers barons also functioned as less than formal lending enterprises for black entrepreneurs serving the African American community through fully legitimate businesses (at a time when blacks suffered severe discrimination in acquiring business loans). These racketeers won further community acceptance through supporting community events and causes—like black sports teams. In fact, Greenlee well understood that black baseball in the early 1930s lacked legitimate profitability. Convincing other black entrepreneurs—legal or otherwise—to invest would mean a kind of civic obligation on their part.

"Unhappy and trapped" by the barriers to white baseball and by the unsettling lack of professionalism in the Negro Leagues, Robinson's doubt and dismay grew exponentially in his several months with the Monarchs. He "began to wonder why I should dedicate my life to a career where the boundaries for progress were set by racial discrimination." Robinson actually threatened to quit the Monarchs several times, with only the personal pleas of teammate and star Hilton Smith stopping him on one of those moments. On the other hand, there were few employment options open to black men in general, and especially to one whose life had revolved around sports. The escalating absences from Rachel, whose "patience was thinning," only added to Robinson's exasperation. "If I left baseball, where could I go, what could I do to earn enough money to help my mother and to marry Rachel?"

In early April 1945, black journalist Joe Bostic, long frustrated by white baseball's feeble excuses for excluding African American talent, took matters into his own hands by bringing two Negro League players to the Brooklyn Dodgers training camp. Having "gotten all the mileage out of conversation" that was possible, he was ready to take "the bull by its horns" and push the black players and their skills directly in front of white baseball owners and managers without waiting for an invitation. "There was this smooth 'out' that you can't accuse baseball of their having a color line or prejudice, because no one had tried." Bostic had even struggled to get black players to agree to the initiative. "You'd be surprised at the number of players who were actually afraid to buck the establishment." Bostic had settled on Dave "Showboat" Thomas, whom he regarded as "the best fielding first baseman" in the country "bar none," and pitcher Terris McDuffie. Bostic knew that McDuffie's finest days might be waning, but he chose him for another reason: "McDuffie had all the guts in the world. Nothing scared him."

The move was decidedly unwelcome for Brooklyn Dodgers owner Branch Rickey. Rickey would play a heralded role in integrating baseball the following year, but on this occasion, "Rickey went berserk almost, with fury," Bostic recalls. The owner deeply resented the publicly difficult position Bostic had forced on him. In words that echoed those of overly cautious southern white moderates during the civil rights campaigns to come in the next two decades, Rickey admonished Bostic. "I'm more for your cause than anybody else, but you are making a mistake using force. You are defeating your own aims." Claiming that whether he agreed or not to give the players an audition, "you'd have the biggest sports story of the century. Either way, it is an embarrassing situation for me and the Brooklyn Dodgers." The Dodgers' owner furthermore smelled a "sickening red tinge" behind the incident, since Bostic worked for Harlem's *People's Voice*, a communist newspaper. The connection was no small matter to the lifelong fervid anticommunist. Rickey, in fact, never forgave the writer for the alleged breach of etiquette, refusing to speak to Bostic until his dying day.

On this spring day, Branch Rickey appeared to be just one more brick in the wall of white supremacy. Surely Bostic could not have known that the headstrong Rickey himself would later produce perhaps the "biggest sports story of the century"—but always on his own terms.

CHAPTER FOUR

~

"A Badge of Martyrdom"

Robinson's Entry into White Baseball

Branch Rickey's elevated umbrage at Joe Bostic's staged tryout of two black players stands in apparent stark contrast to the legend of Rickey unlocking the gates to America's game in the following year. Yet the story highlights the myriad apparent contradictions that lay at the core of the colorful legend of the Dodgers owner. Reared in a devout Methodist home, he appeared to adhere to sacrosanct principle and moralism. "I try to be both a consistent ballplayer and a consistent Christian," he avowed during his early playing days to a baseball beat writer presumably interested only in his swing. At the same time, Rickey loved nothing more than public attention and a dollar: both "Phineas T. Barnum and [famed early twentieth century evangelist] Billy Sunday," according to *Time* magazine. While the much older Rickey refused to break the Sunday Sabbath to attend his Dodgers games, "he was always at the cash box on Monday to count the gate receipts," noted one observer. Those tempted to see the obsessive baseball genius as a one-note traditional sports mind were surprised to learn that he had earned a law degree as a young man and taught Shakespeare, German, and Greek drama during his two-year coaching tenure at Allegheny College.

His relationship with players only added to his contradictory persona. On the one hand, Rickey saw his role as a baseball man in almost missionary terms. "I offered mill hands, plowboys, and high school kids a better way of life. They rose on sandlots to big city diamonds. In a month they earned more than they could have earned in a year. And no young man who signed a contract with me has ever suffered—educationally or morally. If he chose to remain in school, I helped him. When he quit the Cardinal chain, he had

43

learned the lesson of 'clean living' and moral stamina." His pious Midwestern farm parents had named him Wesley Branch Rickey—his legal first name a reference to the revered founder of Methodism (John Wesley) and his middle name a tribute to the biblical passage stating "there shall come forth a rod out of the stem of Jesse, and a Branch shall grow." His regular religious and moral musings earned him the nicknames "the Deacon" and "the Mahatma."

On the other hand, he might tolerate, even encourage, the animated antics of a winning team—a prime example being his early 1930s St. Louis Cardinals "Gas House Gang," legendary for their less than sacrosanct exploits both on and off the diamond. While naming them the "best team I ever had," even the publically moralistic Rickey called the group "a high class team, with nine heavy drinkers." Professing the strictest ethical standards, he was also an extremely savvy businessman. While sportswriter Red Smith agreed that Rickey likely would never lie, "he was so good at evasion, a circumlocution," Smith recalled, "that he didn't have to lie."

Rickey's colorful nature always provided good newspaper copy. So skilled was the cigar-chomping Dodgers owner at spinning yarns and promotional pronouncements that reporters took to calling his press conference room "the cave of winds." But it was his actions on payday that drew some fire. *New York Daily News* sports editor Jimmy Powers ran relentless criticism of Rickey in his 1940s columns on Rickey's skinflint reputation for players' salaries. It was Powers who coined one of the lasting pejoratives for Rickey: "El Cheapo." He was, said Powers, a "tight-fisted man who paid his players coolie salaries."

At less public moments, however, Rickey could be surprisingly generous. Hearing that his Ohio Wesleyan University classmate Don Beach's bank went under during the Great Depression, Rickey wired him immediately: "I need you in St. Louis. How soon can you come?" He promptly awarded Beach a job in Columbus, and employed him for years to come. When Beach's daughter lacked the resources for a college education, Rickey relinquished his own daughter's scholarship monies to the girl. Cardinals catcher Bill DeLancey's 1936 tuberculosis diagnosis serves as another example. Despite his physical incapacities, Rickey continued his salary and created a new Arizona affiliate explicitly so that the ailing DeLancey could work as manager. DeLancey told friends before his death ten years later that Rickey had become a substitute father figure through it all.

Whatever one makes of these different sides of Branch Rickey, there was no mistaking his impact on baseball. A man of relentless passion for improving his club and the game itself, his declining health caused a series of doctors to demand he slow down. Even after retiring as the Pittsburgh Pirates general manager in 1955, he refused to heed that medical advice, asking, "You expect me to do nothing? I did nothing for three days. I never was so tired in all my life." To another doctor's plea for more rest, Rickey had responded, "I certainly expect my funeral cortege to move at a dignified pace."

His genius began with a renowned eye for talent. Sportswriter Jim Murray claimed he "could recognize a great player from the window of a moving train." But he also knew how to nurture and structure his collected talent in new and extraordinary ways. He refined baseball to a developed science, which he obsessively taught to his players. In his first year as a manager, one reporter dubbed him "a Professor of Baseball. His efficiency courses in sliding, baserunning and batting mark a departure in the game." The elements of those "courses," however, soon became staples of America's pasttime. Rickey was the architect of the farm system (which tied Minor League clubs and their players to a Major League franchise) so widely used today by all Major League teams to develop their talent. So important was the innovation that one expert estimated that three out of eight 1949 Major Leaguers had originated in Rickey's farm system alone. A glance across Major League executive offices might have brought a similar conclusion, as many of the game's most acclaimed executives got their start under a Rickey tutelage. While most teams were cutting back during World War II, Rickey ingeniously did the reverse, building a foundation for postwar greatness. He began to collect and sign as much young talent as possible, who populated his rapidly growing number of farm clubs. Like a shark that must keep moving or die, Rickey understood the need to continue to evolve to remain on top: "You have two years to stay ahead of your competition when you come up with a new idea in baseball."

After short stints as a professional player, Branch Rickey had begun his Major League management career in 1914. Starting as a field manager for the St. Louis Browns, Rickey later moved into front office roles with the team and then their crosstown rivals, the St. Louis Cardinals (with whom he won six pennants and four world championships). By 1942, however, Rickey had worn out his welcome with Cardinals owner Sam Breadon, and he left for the presidency of the Brooklyn Dodgers club. Shortly after taking over, he met with Dodgers owner George McLaughlin to float the idea of signing a Negro player. With attendance down, Major League talent depleted by war service abroad, and the Dodgers overstocked with aging players, the time was right for a bold move that would put the team on the map and position them for a strong run in the postwar years. By being the first willing to take the leap, after all, they would furthermore have first pick of a massive pool of untapped athletic talent in the Negro Leagues. McLaughlin, a business-savvy banker, seemed to bite on the idea, but cautioned Rickey, "If you're doing this to improve the ball club, go ahead, but if you're doing it for the emancipation of the Negro, then forget it."

While there is no question that the profit motive had much to do with Rickey's impulse to cross the color line, the always complicated Dodgers president had more principled motivations entangled into the plan as well. If some scoffed at Rickey's occasional moralistic pronouncements, the tendency also led him down the road to play a pivotal role in bringing an African American into the world of white baseball in 1947.

What the wellspring of that motivation was has produced significant speculation. After all, Rickey had shown no discernable hint of interest in integrating the game before his New York arrival. While certainly less than an earthquake, there were a few rumblings of racial progressivism that can be found in Rickey's life before Jackie Robinson strode into his Brooklyn office. As a college student eager to supplement his income in 1907, for example, Rickey's church-going farm boy upbringing had drawn him naturally to work for the Young Men's Christian Association (YMCA). While functioning there as the coordinator for speakers, he took the bold move of inviting the African American leader Booker T. Washington. Rickey's children were certainly subjected to their father's preaching on racial injustice during family meals, including some spirited discussions of Gunnar Myrdal's influential *An American Dilemma* (which celebrated America's legacy to democratic idealism while noting its disparity with racial practices). Daughter Jane recalls an instructive moment when she appeared in traffic court at age sixteen. While proceeding to the courtroom, her father interceded when he saw St. Louis police harshly interrogating a black suspect. Branch Rickey became so unnerved by the racist badgering that he "busted right in on the grilling. He just didn't want to see the guy mistreated; he was a lawyer and he knew people had rights and he wanted to see to it that this guy had someone there for him." Rickey gave the black stranger his card, which the subsequently released man used to acquire a job as Rickey's chauffeur.

By 1943, Branch Rickey had begun to read widely on the issue of race in America. He sampled Lincoln's writings, books on slavery in Brazil and the United States, as well as *An American Dilemma*. But far more important to the lore Rickey promulgated for his actions was an incident that occurred in 1904.

As a young baseball coach for Ohio Wesleyan University, Rickey had a vicarious encounter with racism that "haunted me for many years." Shepherding his weary young men to their hotel the night before a scheduled game with famed Notre Dame University, Rickey arrived to find a scheduling problem. The desk clerk did indeed have the recorded reservation, but certainly not one for the lone African American player. Providing Wesleyan's first baseman Charlie Thomas with a room would violate segregation policy. After much discussion, the management allowed Thomas to reside in Rickey's room on a pullout cot. This proved palatable to hotel staff since such arrangements were often made for black servants traveling with white customers. This satisfied Rickey, but young Thomas was shaken, and late at night—as Rickey would later recount the famous story—Thomas sat on his cot, rubbing at his hands as he sobbed and lamented repeatedly, "Damned black skin! If only I could make them white." It was then, said Rickey, that he "vowed that I would always do whatever I could to see that other Americans did not have to face the bitter humiliation that was heaped upon Charlie Thomas."

While certainly based on a real incident, the legendary tale bears all the markings of the storytelling embellishments of the master of the "cave of winds." Rickey told slightly different versions of it over the years, and Thomas himself dubbed the Deacon's account "exaggerated." Entirely factual or not, the rendering tells us as much about Rickey and his evolving desire to promote principle as an explanation for integrating the game as it reveals Rickey's commitment to attack racism in his corner of the sports world.

It becomes impossible to untangle the practical from the principled reasons for Rickey's move. A review of his own statements suggests that he was first driven primarily by pragmatism in integrating the game, and he gradually shifted to claim social equality had been the goal (particularly as such a claim became more socially acceptable in subsequent years). In the early years after Robinson's Dodger introduction, there are ample examples of Rickey disavowing any intention beyond the practical: a more competitive team that would assure more gate receipts. In a speech just two months before signing Robinson, Rickey used the 1919 constitutional amendment on Prohibition as an instructive justification for caution on racial matters: "Advancement in racial freedoms has doubtless seemed slow . . . [but,] in our effort to be progressive and secure for ourselves our prosperity, we must indeed give consideration to the possibility of untimeliness, the sheer inopportunism—the sad cost of an overreaching experiment. Let us not attempt what cannot be held if gained." When his new black recruit prepared for his first training camp with the Dodgers, Rickey noted that he "can't help his color," and applauded that he "doesn't push it, [is] not responsible for it, [and] isn't insistent that everyone should talk to him as an equal." As late as 1950 (three years after Robinson arrived in the white Majors), Rickey argued that racial improvement could only come through gradual social acceptance (and not government action). "Let Time be, and become, a more potent ally for change," he wrote the conservative publisher of the *Nashville Banner*. "As I see it, legislative force can delay rather than accelerate the solution." While that might seem to undergird the importance of his own action in the Dodgers front office, he downplayed his role in that societal transformation in the same letter: "I did not employ a Negro because he was a Negro, nor did I have in mind at all doing something for the Negro race, or even bringing up that issue. I simply wanted to win a pennant."

By 1955, Rickey maintained that such simple explanations—that breaking baseball's color line due to practical, competitive concerns—were "not really a statement of the whole truth." He began to tell the Charlie Thomas story widely. He had really dreamed of breaking the sport's color line as early as the 1930s, he claimed in a 1956 interview. "The utter injustice of it always was in my mind." If true, one must grapple with a Branch Rickey running a professional sports franchise for many years in St. Louis with nary a move to make good on his supposed profound transformation in a 1904 hotel. On the other hand, publicly deemphasizing a hidden idealism in the early years of his "great experiment" could have been a partial attempt to avoid additional community concern (i.e., to reassure conflicted whites that this integration could be restricted to the ball fields, and was not meant to launch some wider challenge to the racial status quo). In the end, an easy explanation for this complicated man's motivations remains tantalizingly out of reach—especially for someone so skilled at crafting public statements to manipulate the public and the press.

Not all the pressure to make this move was internal, however. Unmistakable was the surrounding social context for racial change as well. In addition to the war causing many to reconsider the color line, there was public pressure from black and white sportswriters to stop baseball segregation. The April 1945 unsuccessful tryouts (with the Dodgers and Red Sox) were signs of the ratcheting up of expectations. Major League Baseball itself formed a commission in the same month to look at the possibility of integration (the commission eventually ground to a slow and actionless end some months later). Mounting political and social leverage hit particularly close to home. As Rickey secretly prepared for change, New York City mayor Fiorello La Guardia was running an Anti-Discrimination Committee to push for baseball integration, and the New York state legislature had just passed a bill to prohibit racial discrimination in hiring.

While these factors no doubt had their effect on the Dodgers president, it is instructive to note how unyielding his front office counterparts were. An illustrative example is the New York Yankees president Larry MacPhail. "You damn professional do-gooders know nothing about baseball," MacPhail had told those pushing for integrating the game. "You're just trying to stir up trouble." Claiming that no black players "would qualify to play in organized baseball," McPhail insisted that baseball must be run as a business. Recognizing that ending Negro League Baseball would also end a cash cow for many white clubs, he reminded, "I rented my ballparks to colored clubs this year, and the rental money is the profit I am able to pay my stockholders." In a sign that pressure was growing, however, many blacks chose the sidewalk instead of the ticket booth as opening day dawned at Yankee Stadium in 1945. Picketing outside the ballpark, the protesters carried signs that read, "If we can pay, why can't we play?" Unfazed, McPhail boasted, "I have no hesitancy in saying that the Yankees have no intention of signing Negro players. . . . It is unfortunate that groups of professional political and social drumbeaters are conducting pressure campaigns in an attempt to force major-league clubs to sign Negro players."

A notable, racially progressive exception that might have tantalizingly beat the bold Branch Rickey to the punch was Bill Veeck. A great showman and businessman not afraid to rock the boat to earn a dollar, Veeck had already rescued the last-place Minor League Milwaukee team by innovating with fireworks displays and free beer. By 1943, he had turned his ambitious sights on buying a Major League franchise: the Philadelphia Phillies. Equally floundering as had been the Milwaukee team, his secret plan was to recruit several or more black players to Philadelphia as "the only untapped reservoir" of talent available to boost the team's flagging fortunes. Veeck, though, made a fatal mistake: notifying Major League Baseball commissioner Landis before he bought the club. Landis, remembered Veeck, "wasn't exactly shocked but he wasn't exactly overjoyed either." Still, Veeck left the commissioner's Chicago office eager to finalize the purchase, having completed this professional courtesy. What awaited Veeck the next morning in Philadelphia shocked him. The Phillies owner had hurriedly turned the team over to the stewardship of National League president Ford Frick, who in turn sold it to a lumber dealer for half of Veeck's offered price. The Phillies waited fourteen more years before a black player wore their uniform. Veeck, however, completed his scheme in just four, with his newly purchased Cleveland Indians in July 1947 (three months after Robinson had pioneered the path).

However one accounts for Branch Rickey's motives, he was ready to begin his slow, secretive plan to integrate America's game in May 1945. Rickey announced what appeared to be a significant event: his plan to join the new "well-organized, legitimate Negro league" to be named the United States League (created just five months prior). Long dismissive of the current Negro Leagues as "rackets" run by criminally suspect owners who did not provide proper structure and professionalism, this new entity, he claimed, would provide regular scheduling, more legally binding contracts, and better treatment for the players. (In a lengthy aside, he further claimed that the two recent black player tryouts into which the Red Sox and Dodgers had been pressured were a Communist conspiracy to incite unnecessary racial turmoil.) The news reached hostile ears among many white Major League owners, who already had established profitable rental relationships with Negro League clubs. Washington Senators owner Clark Griffith claimed Rickey was "attempting to destroy two well-organized leagues . . . in which colored people of this country have faith and confidence." The African American press poorly received this, seeing the United States League as a lose-lose proposition (lose black ownership of some of the teams and still not integrate the game). One black paper restated the strong desire to have black players in the Majors, "but we won't have any major-league owners running any segregated leagues for us." Another fumed, "When I left that meeting . . . I had formed the opinion that it would be a hot day in December before Rickey would ever have a Negro wear the uniform of" a white Major League team.

Unbeknownst to the gathered press was Rickey's additional hidden plan to use the new league—and his own Brown Dodgers team—as a pretext primarily to scout and recruit African American players, not for a Negro league, but for his white team. The Dodgers president, though, remained maddeningly mum about the subterfuge. "The baseball people were the very last ones that I wished to know anything about it," he later claimed. "If the United States League succeeded on a permanent basis, well and good. That result, however, was incidental to my main purpose. . . . [T]he fundamental objective . . . was to enable me to do open scouting, with experienced men, in the Negro field."

Provided with the smokescreen of his new Brown Dodgers organization, Rickey set about the work of finding the best black talent available. His scouts scattered across the country to eye Negro League prospects. From the beginning, Rickey was evaluating not just athletic prowess but character and mettle as well. "I had to get a man who would carry the burden on the field," he later recounted. "I needed a man to carry the badge of martyrdom. The press had to accept him. He had to stimulate a good reaction of the Negro race itself, for an unfortunate one might have solidified the antagonism of other colors. And, I had to consider the attitude of the man's teammates."

Indeed, noted black journalist Carl Rowan concurred that picking "the wrong Negro would be calamitous." A black candidate who failed at the experiment would confirm naysayers' arguments that neither black players nor the white teammates and public were ready, closing the door long after to further integration trials. Not only must he be a "virtual cinch to succeed on the field," but the player must be "a clean-living family man whose character was above reproach" since he "would find himself besieged by white women eager to give him their affections. The image of Jack Johnson and his three white wives was always before" Rickey and his white fellow executives.

Satchel Paige and Josh Gibson were the first names to emerge, but Rickey thought them too old for the project. The player, he conjectured, would likely need to spend at least a few years in the white Minor Leagues before being called up to the big leagues, and the older specimens' skills might badly diminish before arriving with the Dodgers. Furthermore, both failed the Deacon's morals test due to their off-the-field indulgences. Known as womanizers, Rickey characterized Gibson's extracurricular behavior in particular as "not encouraging." Other names that emerged also came with problems: outfielder Monte Irvin had yet to be dismissed from war service, catcher Roy Campanella's easy-going demeanor was thought to be missing the inner fire required to contend with the sure racist onslaught, and the young pitcher Don Newcombe lacked the necessary maturity to weather the storm. That left a twenty-six-year-old Kansas City Monarchs infielder by the name of Jackie Robinson.

While Robinson fit Rickey's profile in athletic talent and youth, there were problems, he was told. Robinson had had his scrapes with the law, both as a youth and an army man. He also had a tendency toward aggression and unsettling outspokenness. As Rickey plumbed these reports, he was mindful also of a fundamental dilemma in his black prospect. The player would need to withhold much of his anger on the field to win white hearts and minds, but he had to do so while maintaining his own sense of his righteousness and determination. "How can a man of worth and human dignity and unsullied personality bend enough?" Rickey later wondered. "How could a man with distinctive personality successfully keep it unscraped with constant absorption of attacks calculated to absorb his self-respect?" Even Rickey acknowledged that "[t]here were just not very many such humans" who fit the bill.

Hence, Rickey found many of the supposed negatives on Robinson to be surprisingly helpful commodities in the project ahead. As future African American teammate Don Newcombe put it, "He was the kind of man who had to make his presence felt. He sometimes overdid it," especially in response to racism. "Like a boiler, he could not keep it all inside him." Rickey astutely noted, however, "If he had done the things people are criticizing him for as a white player, he would have been praised to the skies as a fighter, a holler guy, a real competitor, a ballplayer's ballplayer. But because he's black his aggressiveness is offensive to some white people." In fact, when hearing of Robinson's court martial and its circumstances, Rickey saw not a difficult malcontent, but "a man of ideals—a battler."

Resolved to leave no stone unturned, Rickey traveled personally to Los Angeles to explore stories of the player's youth and college years. He learned that the teenaged Robinson had run-ins with local police because he was constantly "shootin' off his mouth about his constitutional rights." There were reports that he had altercations with coaches, players, and officials, that he was a "racial agitator." Even the sympathetic columnist Will Connolly reported, "He wasn't the most popular man on the campus and off. Jackie had a genius for getting into extracurricular scrapes." Rickey investigated this further with African American sportswriter Wendell Smith, with whom he had begun to develop a confidence, inquiring whether "Jackie was a belligerent type of individual. I didn't want to tell Mr. Rickey, 'Yes, he's tough to get along with,'" remembered Smith. "A lot of us knew that. When he was aroused he had a sizable temper. But to survive, he couldn't be a Mickey Mouse." A fellow Negro Leaguer, Gene Benson, who found Robinson to be "a swell person" once they became barnstorming roommates, recalled initially hearing the widespread stories of his teammate being "controversial" and his reputation for getting "involved in fisticuffs all the time."

Still, there was no mistaking the impression left by his athletic prowess, nor the pleasing reports of his moral makeup. Neither a drinker nor smoker, he emerged as a "clean-living young man who didn't run around with girls." Furthermore, Rickey, the always brilliant evaluator of talent, may have seen in Robinson's edge just the ingredient necessary for his bold experiment. After all, he would need to be determined enough to stand toe to toe with white supremacy. Hence, Rickey needed "to have a boy with some aggressiveness, with some guts, because he's got to be bold and gritty enough to stand up inflinchingly." And so it was that the Dodgers executive staked his reputation on what others had called a "smart guy whose major fault is that he likes to argue with white folks."

Since the Monarchs infielder's name had emerged a number of times, Rickey sent his most reliable scout to see for himself. Jackie Robinson looked up in late August 1945 to see his future sitting in the bleachers in the guise of a retired journeyman catcher who was now Rickey's trusted assistant: Clyde Sukeforth. Rickey had sent his man to see the African American prospect for himself during the Monarchs' series in Chicago. Should Sukeforth be satisfied that rumors of an inadequate infield throwing arm were misguided, he was to bring the young shortstop back to Brooklyn to meet the Mahatma. If, however, Robinson's "schedule won't permit it, if he can't come in, then make an appointment for me and I'll go out there."

By now, Sukeforth had logged quite a number of miles in pursuit of talent allegedly for Rickey's Brown Dodgers team. Like virtually everyone else, his boss had not informed him of a hidden purpose for scouting black players. This time, though, Sukeforth smelled something far more provocative in his instructions. "Mr. Rickey go out there?" the scout later questioned. "To see if some guy named Robinson was good enough to play shortstop for the Brooklyn Brown Bombers? Well, I'm not the smartest guy in the world, but I said to myself, this could be the real thing." When he approached Robinson, of course, he nonetheless maintained the ruse that he was recruiting for a Negro team. The young black player, who had already endured innumerable obstacles to find his place in the world, faced one more: Sukeforth had arrived to see him with an injured shoulder. Despite the wounded wing, Sukeforth decided to proceed with the Brooklyn meeting. As it turned out, Robinson's injury proved an ironic asset by providing him the recovery time off from the Monarchs to make the journey.

That night in Chicago, an astute Robinson peppered Sukeforth with questions, seemingly suspect that his trip to Brooklyn was about more than joining another Negro team. "Why is Mr. Rickey interested in my arm? Why does he want to see me?" And, most importantly, Robinson lingered over the meaning of Rickey's offer to come see Robinson himself. "The significance of that last part wasn't lost on him. I could see that," recalled Sukeforth. As they traveled east by train, Sukeforth was already intrigued by Rickey's selection. "There was something about that man that just gripped you. He was tough, he was intelligent, and he was proud."

After their rail arrival in New York, Sukeforth ushered the young athlete into Rickey's walnut-paneled office with polite introductions, but "the old man was so engrossed in Robinson by that time he didn't hear a damn word I said," the scout recalled. "When [Rickey] met somebody he was interested in, he studied them in the most profound way. He just stared and stared. And that's what he did with Robinson—stared at him as if he were trying to get inside the man. And Jack stared right back at him. Oh, they were a pair, those two! I tell you, the air in that office was electric." Robinson, under this penetrating gaze, "felt almost naked."

Robinson recalls that Rickey broke the silence with a surprising first question: "You got a girl?" Robinson explained the tenuousness of his physical separation from Rachel, but Rickey suggested, "When we get through today you may want to call her up because there are times when a man needs a woman by his side." Having both indicated his intrusion into the player's personal conduct and the gravity of the interview, Rickey now sprung his integration plan on the visitor. Robinson's "reactions seemed like some kind of weird mixture churning in a blender. I was thrilled, scared, and excited. I was incredulous." "I want to win the pennant and we need ball players," Rickey intoned. "Do you think you can do it?"

Robinson's affirmative answer set off a barrage of challenges by Rickey, aimed at testing the player's psychological suitability to be the face of the Mahatma's grand experiment. Could the black man hold up under the strain? "I know you're a good ballplayer," Rickey asserted. "What I don't know is whether you have the guts." The "heat coming up into my cheeks," Robinson bristled at the Dodgers executive "questioning my courage" and perhaps needing assurance as to whether "I was a coward." As to whether the line of questioning meant the Dodgers were "looking for a Negro who is afraid to fight back," the executive retorted, "I'm looking for a ballplayer with guts enough not to fight back." To underscore his point dramatically, Rickey pulled open his desk drawer to read from his beloved, dog-eared copy of Giovanni Papini's *Life of Christ*. The 1921 tome had long been such a Rickey personal and inspirational favorite that he gave copies to all his children one Christmas. On this occasion, he returned to Papini's passage highlighting Jesus's nonviolent nature and his exhortation to "turn the other cheek" upon an assailant—a trait he would emphasize as a vital tool for breaking baseball's color line.

Rickey went on to deluge his prospective signee with racist encounters he would likely endure, acting many of them out for emphasis and to test Robinson's mettle: the racist hotel clerk, the railroad conductor, restaurateur, fan, umpire, and—most especially—the physical and psychological challenges of opposing white players. Swinging his fist an inch away from Robinson's face in imitation of a hostile opponent, Rickey shouted, "Tarbaby! Dirty black son of a bitch!" At one point, the Dodgers president removed his jacket, sprawled on the floor, and proceeded to mimic a prejudiced white base runner with a high-sliding spiked cleat deliberately rammed into his leg, taunting, "How do you like that nigger boy?" Rickey's red-faced dramatics became so convincing that Robinson took to "chain-gripping my fingers behind my back" to contain his rage. In a more modern context, the notion of a white man educating and testing a black man on the trials and tribulations of white supremacy would surely be received as unendurably, appallingly paternalistic. But this was 1945, and Robinson no doubt understood that Rickey's performance was a necessary bridge to a better life.

Rickey later avowed to reporters that all baseball players "look as like to me as doorbells" and that he "never notice[d] the color of their skins. I never meant to be a crusader, and I hope I won't be regarded as one. My purpose is to be fair to all people. My one selfish objective is to win ballgames." Surely Rickey's protestations to pigment blindness indicated his desire to move beyond the abiding color line that had divided America since its inception. But in hindsight, it seems clear that Rickey was either deluding himself or creating another of his famous sweeping public pronouncements to sway the gathered press. It is doubtful that Rickey would have interrogated young Robinson so heavily on his character and family background if his skin were white. In Rickey's mind, Robinson's race had made great caution necessary in overcoming lingering white perceptions of blacks' innate immorality. Rickey had clearly looked for far more than athletic talent in this roster slot. Surely no white players had sat in the Dodgers president's office for hours enduring mock abuse. Surely no white players had made personal pledges to abide by the biblical directive to turn the other cheek. Furthermore, the Deacon's claims that profit was the beginning and end to his machinations in integrating the game is also misleading. He clearly was a crusader. By his own admission, he had solemnly vowed to save other blacks from the "bitter humiliation" endured by Charlie Thomas weeping on his hotel cot.

Still, the determined athlete held his tongue and temper until Rickey was satisfied that the pledge of nonretaliation would be kept. Robinson was likewise satisfied that the Dodgers president was sufficiently committed to the enterprise that he would ride the rocky waters with the player. "We can't fight our way through this," Rickey contended. "We've got no army. There's virtually nobody on our side. No owners, no umpires, very few newspapermen. . . . We can win only if we can convince the world that I'm doing this because you're a great ballplayer, a fine gentleman." Ultimately, despite Robinson's uncertainty over holding firm to nonviolence, "I knew that I must. I had to do it for so many reasons. For black youth, for my mother, for Rae, for myself." He even conceded he had "begun to feel I had to do it for Branch Rickey."

Thus, after a grueling three-hour interview, Rickey retrieved an already prepared contract to play for the Dodgers' Montreal farm team in the 1946 season. He also retrieved a pledge from Robinson to keep the matter a secret until Rickey's planned revelation to the media later that year. One fascinating mystery remains from the meeting: whether Rickey extracted Robinson's commitment to avoid angry confrontations indefinitely, or—as some later claimed—to hold the pledge only his first two years in a Dodgers uniform (after which the black athlete's position would presumably be secure in white baseball). Some claimed that the Jackie Robinson they saw beyond the first two Major League seasons would far more resemble the defiant man who was court martialed and dubbed a "racial agitator" during his college years.

In late October 1945, the Dodgers' farm affiliate in Montreal introduced their new African American recruit to reporters' "stunned silence." Robinson would begin there in a more racially moderate atmosphere, and hope to work his way to the Major League level in short order. Far less silent was the American public reaction to the white leagues' color line being crossed. Branch Rickey Jr., who functioned as the Dodgers' farm system director, sought to hedge against the certain criticism the Dodgers could expect: "[Montreal Royals President] Mr. Racine and my father undoubtedly will be criticized in some sections of the United States where racial prejudice is rampant. They are not inviting trouble, but they won't avoid it if it comes. . . . It may cost the Brooklyn organization a number of ballplayers. Some of them, particularly if they come from certain sections of the South, will steer away from a club with Negro players on its roster. Some players now with us may even quit, but they'll be back in baseball after they work a year or two in a cotton mill."

Having established a defensive posture, the incoming fire from much of white America was swift and sure. Former infielder Bill Werber took umbrage at Rickey Jr.'s shot at southern players who would be asked, after all, "to accept socially and to play with a Negro" in the Dodgers' "highly distasteful" integration project. Werber found Rickey's singling out of southern players "a definite insult to every southern boy." White journalists added to the criticism. The Sporting News sized up Robinson as having the talent "which, were he white, would make him eligible for a trial with . . . the Dodgers'

"I cannot face my God much longer knowing that His black creatures are held separate and distinct from His white creatures in the game that has given me all that I can call my own."

Dodger boss Rickey realized a lifelong ambition when he broke baseball's color line by signing Jackie Robinson (below). Behind Rickey is a picture of Abe Lincoln.

A Branch Grows in Brooklyn

Jackie Robinson

Branch Rickey flourishes in Flatbush, champions the Negro in baseball, and is the father of major league's profitable farm system

By TIM COHANE

Wesley Branch Rickey, 64-year-old president of the Brooklyn Dodgers, enjoys an indifferent press. Some sportswriters roar regularly for his head to be brought in on home plate, preferably with a baseball in his mouth as a gag in the literal sense. Others are less bloodthirsty.

"Branch has so got into the habit of quoting scripture," these latter point out, "that even when his mo-

tives are purely altruistic, his critics are still dubious."

Most Tongmen and Pollyannas alike, however, hailed Rickey in print or in private when he brought the Negro into modern organized baseball for the first time recently by signing Jackie Robinson, a shortstop, to a contract with the Dodgers' farm team at Montreal.

Nobody could reasonably suspect materialistic motives. Negro stars are not imperative to the pennant Rickey labors toward, nor could they improve attendance at Ebbets Field where a third-place team played to over a million paying fans last season.

In fact, signing Robinson may cost Rickey money, and Branch is about as allergic to money as he is to Rickey. Already, talent bird dogs have routed young prospects away from Brooklyn, because (Continued on page 72)

Figure 4.1. 1946 *Look* magazine article featuring Brooklyn Dodgers president Branch Rickey and his signing of Jackie Robinson. *Source*: Library of Congress, http://www.loc.gov/pictures/item/97519248

Class B farm [team] at Newport News." *Daily News* columnist Jimmy Powers regarded Robinson's shot as "1,000 to 1," and ridiculed Rickey's alleged progressivism as inspired by a "heart as big as a watermelon." San Francisco sportswriter Will Connolly resurrected the rumors that had emerged during Rickey's scouting when he warned the Dodgers owner that his selection was indeed a "troublemaker." Not to be left out, southern cotton mill owners found reason for offense, threatening to sue for Rickey Jr's insult to their industry.

Those inside the game were also less than delighted. Minor League Baseball Commissioner William Bramham opined, "Whenever I hear a white man . . . protesting what a friend he is to the Negro race, right then I know the Negro needs a bodyguard." Bramham had seen Rickey's "carpetbagger" type before who took the "guise of helping" to use "the Negro for their selfish interests, who retard the race." Baseball great Rogers Hornsby spoke for many white Major Leaguers when he cautioned, "Ballplayers on the road live close together . . . [I]t won't work." Pitcher Bob Feller "couldn't foresee any future for Robinson in big league baseball." Robinson had "football shoulders" that would prevent a properly smooth swing. "If he were a white man I doubt if they would even consider him as big league material."

Cleveland sportswriter Ed Macauley had a more nuanced assessment. The sympathetic journalist questioned whether baseball was the best place to launch the integration experiment. Since American racial problems were "an aspect of a grave social question," he worried that baseball teams and their players "seldom operated on the highest level of mental maturity" and hence weren't "the places to seek the answer" to such an important issue.

More complicated was the reaction of African Americans to the news. Some, like Negro American League president J. B. Martin, enthusiastically welcomed Robinson's signing, claiming to speak for "the sentiment of 15 million Negroes in America who are with [Rickey] one hundred per cent. [We] will always remember the day and date of this great event." But others who celebrated also saw the gravity of the moment. Black journalist Edgar T. Rouzeau worried that "the hopes and anxieties of the Negro race were placed squarely on [Robinson's] shoulders." The news, he wrote, "was received in Harlem with a mixture of joy and trepidation." Similarly, Ludlow Werner of the *New York Age* was "happy over the event but I'm sorry for Jackie. He will be haunted by the expectations of his race. To 15,000,000 Negroes he will symbolize not only their prowess in baseball, but their ability to rise to an opportunity. And Lord help him with his fellow Negroes if he should fail them."

African American ballplayers had a comparably mixed response. Before the white press, Satchel Paige was the consummate gentleman, calling Robinson "a number one professional player. They couldn't have picked a better man." But behind his relief that the line had finally been broken, the proud hurler revealed years later being "hurt . . . deep down" over not breaking the barrier himself. "I'd been the guy who started all that big talk about letting us in the big time. . . . I'd been the one the white boys wanted to barnstorm against. I'd been the one everybody said should be in the majors." Paige was not alone. Hilton Smith, another Negro League player, revealed the mixed sentiment of black players left behind when he bitterly noted the accidental nature of the man selected: "It all came down to this; he had played with white boys" at USC. Hall of Famer Monte Irvin conceded "a certain amount of jealousy. . . . There were real stars in the Negro Leagues—Josh Gibson, Satchel Paige, Roy Campanella. Those guys were proven stars. But they said Branch wanted a guy with talent and a college education, able to express himself with the press and in other situations."

Many Negro League owners had a far less complex response to Rickey's actions. What some saw as inspired heroism, they saw as a dishonest violation of Robinson's contract with the Kansas City Monarchs. The question of black players' contractual position was a thorny one. Most Negro League players did sign contracts that bound them to their teams in a fashion similar to the white Major Leagues. Adhering to those legal agreements was another matter, however. "There were regular contracts," Negro League player Bill Yancey remembers. "But we didn't pay much attention to them. You signed up for a year. All right, you played that year but if you felt like jumping the next year, you jumped. There was a reserve clause [binding the player to the team] . . . but it was disregarded. . . . If I was unhappy I said the hell with this and I jumped." Such customs allowed Rickey to proclaim the Negro Leagues as a "racket" whose contracts meant nothing; hence, the Dodgers president offered the Monarchs (who had, after all, given Robinson professional training and a forum to showcase his skills) nothing to reimburse the loss of their shortstop.

Monarchs owner J. L. Wilkinson was especially incensed. He had imagined his Kansas City team to be the most likely candidate for absorption into the Majors. The Monarchs were the top baseball draw west of St. Louis, and an obvious place to expand. Rather than plucking player by player, he had hoped the Major Leagues would simply allow his entire star-studded team to join the heretofore all-white big leagues. Wilkinson's team in time lost more of its roster to the Major Leagues than any other Negro League club (including the likes of Robinson, Satchel Paige, Hank Thompson, Connie Johnson, Willard Brown, Elston Howard, and Ernie Banks). "Rickey is no Abraham Lincoln or FDR," decried Wilkinson, "and we won't accept him as dictator of Negro baseball." Another Monarchs official claimed that Rickey "owes us a moral obligation. Whatever he might have offered would have been okay with us—but [he] . . . was not even gentleman enough to answer or acknowledge my many letters I wrote to him." But the adulation of the black press for Robinson and his new white team undercut Wilkinson's position. Wanting to avoid the perception that he was holding back racial progress, he gradually conceded.

Notably, when the Mexican League lured away one of Rickey's Dodgers a year later, he sued an American sportswriter for allegedly aiding the Mexicans in pilfering his player (to whom Rickey claimed exclusive rights). Rickey lost the case. He lashed out at the time at "Mexican baseball league agents [who] have been damaging the morale of my players by offering them large sums of money to break their contract and play in the Mexican League. I won't stand for it."

While Rickey openly questioned the legal status of Negro League players, Cleveland Indians owner Bill Veeck provided a counter example. Veeck— who had been rebuffed by then Commissioner Landis about possibly bringing in black players in 1943—did compensate the Negro Leagues' Newark Eagles owner Effa Manley $15,000 when he signed Larry Doby away as the first African American baseballer in the American League a few months after Robinson's entry. Manley was not quiet about her anger at Rickey's tactics. "Mr. Rickey tried to take our parks," she intoned years afterward. "But he couldn't take them. I begged the owners of the Negro leagues to try to find out what was on his mind. I felt he was too smart to ignore. He couldn't take our parks, but he did take our ballplayers. He outmaneuvered us completely and the fans deserted us."

After all the talk and tumult over Robinson's signing, there was a still a team to assemble, practice to be done, and games to be played. A ten-week barnstorming tour in Venezuela that winter allowed Robinson a respite from the press scrutiny. A February marriage to longtime sweetheart Rachel Isum brought a more joyful diversion. But come late February 1946, Jackie Robinson readied himself for his moment: spring training with a Major League ball club. For Robinson and his new wife, attending meant crossing the Mason Dixon line into Florida. What remains for many of baseball's fans and white players a romantic place of sunny warmth and frolic was not taken so lightly for African Americans in the 1940s. "I had heard so many stories about the treatment of Negroes in the Deep South that I was bewildered," Rachel Robinson remembers. Furthermore, she had to worry about her husband's behavior, as well, aware as she was of "how quickly Jack's temper could flare up in the face of a racial insult."

When Jackie's mother, Mallie Robinson, said goodbye at the airport to the hopeful young couple, she left them with a shoebox of homemade fried chicken and hard-boiled eggs. No doubt a well-intentioned gesture, the odorous meal nevertheless left her daughter-in-law in a quandary. Carrying the meal aboard a plane, Rachel feared, would mark them as a lower-class black couple—despite Jackie's double-breasted blue suit and her ermine coat just as they sought to showcase themselves as worthy of both a seat on this luxurious mode of travel and the new opportunity that awaited Jackie on arrival. Eager to please, Rachel took the food graciously and made her way to the gate. She would soon discover the wisdom of Mallie's gift.

As a native southerner, Mallie Robinson understood far better than the young idealistic couple that travel through the Jim Crow South often required considerable planning—and backup planning—for African Americans. Any presumption that blacks could easily locate an open door for accommodations and meals along the way was frequently dashed. After an all-night flight from Los Angeles to New Orleans, the Robinsons were told that they were bumped from their connecting flight. In search of food to pass the time, Rachel recalled that her husband "almost exploded" when told that the airport restaurant would not allow them to consume any food purchase at a table. Refusing the indignity of a takeout order, they left to search for a hotel and gratefully gobbled the contents of Mallie's shoebox. It now dawned on them that the condescending white "stereotype about Negro 'picnics' on trains probably grew out of just this kind of situation—Negroes packing a lunch because of knowledge that dining cars and restaurants would refuse them service."

After a night spent "in a filthy, run-down place resembling a flophouse," Rachel Robinson and her husband were again told to exit the plane at the connecting Pensacola flight, which left her "puzzled." Noticing that a Mexican American was also asked to deplane, Jack engaged in a "heated argument with the manager," who had claimed that the three passengers of color must be removed to allow for the loading of more fuel as the plane now headed into a storm. When Jackie observed two white passengers entering the plane, he "protested vociferously," but Rachel "knew that this would be of little avail." "I had been ready to explode with rage," recounted Jackie, "but I knew that the result would mean newspaper headlines about an ugly racial incident and possible arrest not only for me but also for Rae. By giving in to my feelings then, I could have blown the whole major league bit. I had swallowed my pride and choked back my anger."

Now "anxious to be on time" since "the entire sports world" was "watching him and his conduct," Robinson proceeded by bus to Jacksonville. The couple would then be "in for another rude jolt." When white passengers began filling the bus at a later stop, Rachel woke her husband to relay the driver's command to move to the rear, less comfortable "Negro seats" in preference to the white riders. Rachel was "concerned about his reaction, especially given his fight in the army over this very same order. But . . . he docilely led me to the last seat in the rear." A "helpless" feeling filled Jackie as he was far more inclined to "take a beating than to remain passive." Instead, he reminded himself that long ago the couple had "agreed that I had no right to lose my temper and jeopardize the chances of all the blacks who would follow me if I could help break down the barriers." His wife nonetheless felt "a mixed state of disbelief, relief, and pain," and later wept quietly, as her "man had become the white South's 'boy,' in order to keep us safe."

The Robinsons' trial by Jim Crow fire was only beginning. Since the spring training locations of Sanford and Daytona Beach, Florida, enforced segregation, the couple were barred from staying at the hotel assigned to the Dodger organization's white players. Adequate accommodations could only be found at the home of a local black pharmacist and civil rights figure. To ensure that Robinson received proper moral support, Rickey recruited two other African Americans: player John Wright and journalist Wendell Smith. Wright was signed away from the Negro League's Homestead Grays and had compiled impressive numbers as a pitcher—including a 25–4 record in his last year in the Negro Leagues and a victory over the Majors' Chicago White Sox while on a military team during the war. Smith, who remained personally invested in seeing a black player succeed in the Majors, was sent in advance to locate lodging for Jackie and Rachel Robinson. Rickey also put Smith on the payroll throughout spring training to attend to any needs that might arise. That included shadowing the two black athletes, "because," cautioned Rickey, "much harm could come if either of these boys were to do or say something or other out of turn."

Both Wright and Robinson were designated to begin their foray into white baseball with the Dodgers' Montreal farm team, the Royals. This would provide an opportunity for the two to get seasoned in the white Minor Leagues, and the team's Canadian home would give the men a more racially progressive atmosphere. In Florida, however, segregation continued its long reign. Several games, in fact, were canceled due to local officials' objections—one community creatively explained an *afternoon* game cancellation due to a problem with the overhead lights.

As anticipated, Robinson felt an immediate "current of tension" between himself and his teammates—a mood that continued through the camp, as "they made no particular effort to be friendly. They didn't speak to Wright or to me except in the line of duty." His manager would be Mississippian Clay Hopper, who showed no initial "outward sign of prejudice," but whom Robinson later overheard asking Rickey, "Do you really think that a nigger is a human being, Mr. Rickey?" Privately, Hopper revealed his own worries about the impact of the Robinson experiment on himself. "Please don't do this to me," he pleaded with Rickey. "I'm white and I've lived in Mississippi all my life. If you do this, you're going to force me to move my family and my home out of Mississippi." But Rickey remained stalwart, showing up at Montreal practices to demonstrate his public backing, shouting to Robinson, "Go after that pitch! Take a lead! Be bold! Make them worry!" Rachel recalled that "Jack truly needed that support. He was nervous and tense and needed the phone calls; and, they came regularly. . . . Rickey's relationship with Jack became very personal, very intimate. It was paternal—not paternalistic, but paternal."

The game itself also presented challenges for Robinson. Concerns about his arm strength caused the Royals to move him from his traditional position of shortstop to second base, then to first base, before shifting him back to second. This disrupted Robinson's comfort considerably, and it is surely one reason for his poor batting average in camp. A much greater contributor, of course, was the mountain of pressure he carried on behalf of his race. As African American fans cheered him in exhibition games, "I wanted to produce so much that I was tense and over-anxious . . . swinging at bad balls." His determination to prove wrong the concerns about his throwing arm caused him to hurl his plays much harder to first base, until he strained his arm—which affected both his infield defensive plays and his batting swing. The ensuing hitting slump then compounded his nerves as he worried whether his poor plate performances indicated that the Majors were beyond his skills. Rachel recalls the couple being "afraid that Jack simply would not make the team, that he would have to be cut in spring training. Every day without a hit made Rickey's experiment seem more risky." By early April, however, Robinson's swing (and, thus, his confidence as well) had returned—a trend that continued into the Royals' regular season.

With spring training over, Robinson began his Minor League run with the Dodger's AAA affiliate, the Montreal Royals. The Robinsons found the racial climate in their new home of Montreal a refreshing "atmosphere of complete acceptance," recalled Jackie. Soon after moving in, neighboring women arrived to welcome them, even giving the newly pregnant Rachel some of their Canadian food rationing coupons (still being used from the war period) should she require more. They also attended to her when her husband was traveling. The African American couple, as something of an oddity in the French Canadian city, were "stared at on the street," said Robinson. These stares, however, "were friendly," including the local children who lined the streets to see the Royals star leave for games.

The Royals themselves proved a more reticent group. While Robinson's relations with his white teammates were far from hostile, their interactions were largely confined to the ballpark, with Robinson often eating separately from his white colleagues at team meals. Gradually, the team warmed up to him—especially when his contributions to winning became evident. The club manager, Clay Hopper, also took considerable time to warm up to his African American second baseman. Robinson noted that Hopper was "careful to be courteous, but prejudice . . . was deeply ingrained in him." By midseason, the manager admitted to reporters that he "has all the qualifications of a great ballplayer," adding, "if he was white, he'd be a cinch to go anywhere." By season's end, Hopper was confessing to Rickey, "I want to take back what I said to you last spring. I'm ashamed of it. . . . He was not only a great ballplayer good enough for Brooklyn, but also a fine gentleman."

Robinson found Montreal fans to be enthusiastically supportive. Opposing ballparks could be another matter. The Buffalo City Council actually ceremonially presented Robinson with gifts of cash, a wristwatch, and a traveling bag. Other cities were considerably less welcoming. Syracuse players engaged in an unseemly torrent of racist epithets from the dugout, culminating in tossing a black cat onto the field, yelling, "Hey, Jackie, there's your cousin." One trip to Baltimore, the southernmost destination of the Royals' road games, produced a close and physically aggressive final play that led to a brawl at home plate. Fans then cleared the stands to join in the free-for-all. Robinson had already headed for the clubhouse when the melee broke out, but Baltimoreans surrounded the visiting locker room to await his emergence, yelling, "Come out here Robinson, you son of a bitch. We know you're up there. We're gonna get you." "Those fans were there," remembered a white teammate, "until one o'clock in the morning." Three white Royals stayed with Robinson until the crowd thinned, and accompanied him to his hotel.

Such encounters did wear increasingly on Robinson, especially as he struggled to stay true to his agreement with Rickey to bottle his anger. "The toll that incidents like these took was greater than I realized," he later wrote. "I was overestimating my stamina and underestimating the beating I was taking." Added to the grinding racism was the unrelenting "stresses of just knowing that you were pulling a big weight of a whole lot of people on your back," remembered Rachel. "I think Jackie really felt, and I agreed, that there would be serious consequences if he didn't succeed [including] . . . that nobody would try again for a long time." As those strains grew, Robinson struggled to sleep and eat, frequently feeling nauseous. By late August, Rachel and Hopper were so concerned that they urged him to see a physician. The doctor, said Jackie, "was afraid I was going to have a nervous breakdown," and prescribed ten days rest. Given five days off by the Royals, Robinson returned in three when the team went on a brief losing streak. Speculation over the possible cause for the myriad health problems that drove Jackie to his early death at fifty-three has often centered on this unrelenting pressure he endured from the beginning of the integration project.

The now pregnant Rachel Robinson endured her own health concerns, which she concealed from her already overburdened husband. She attended Royals home games religiously. But when her husband traveled to often inhospitable opposing ballparks, she "exhibited symptoms I still don't understand." Three months into her pregnancy, she began having fevers "of undetermined origins" that could climb to a worrisome 104 degrees. "Even the doctors didn't know what to attribute it to." When Jackie returned home, she would return to normal.

If Robinson displayed signs of the psychological burdens off the field, there was little evidence that it affected his play. By the end of the 1946 International League season, Robinson carried the highest batting average, had tied for first in runs scored, had come in second for stolen bases, and ranked the best defensive second baseman to boot. Not surprisingly, those numbers earned him the league's Most Valuable Player award. Even the manager of the opposing Jersey City Giants wished he could "have nine Robinsons. If I had one Jackie, I'd room with him myself and put him to bed nights." More importantly, Robinson's play was a critical factor in the Royals winning the "Little World Series" for the Minor Leagues. When a delirious Montreal crowd rushed the field to lift Robinson on their shoulders at the final game, it was a finally satisfying conclusion to his first difficult year in white baseball.

It caused the *Pittsburgh Courier* to remark, "It was probably the only day in history that a black man ran from a white mob with love instead of lynching on its mind."

One "sour note" for Robinson's season was the fate of pitcher Johnny Wright, who struggled with nerves during spring training outings. After two regular season relief appearances (one shaky and one impressive) and two weeks of riding the bench over a six-week span, Wright was demoted to the Class C Three Rivers organization in Quebec. True to his unassuming demeanor, Wright left without displaying "an inkling of resentment or jealousy," noted black sportswriter Wendell Smith. From the beginning, it seemed, Wright had been handled differently than Robinson. Both Wright and Robinson were married men, but Branch Rickey had not given Wright the same exemption to Dodger spring training rules that he gave Robinson—allowing his wife to attend to steady his nerves. The different standards for the two black players gave credence to the view that Wright was there less as a field contributor than a friendly face for Robinson.

Wright, a lanky twenty-seven-year-old with nine years of professional experience, however, was hardly an average talent. Noted for his excellent control and a nasty curveball, some rated his fastball as stronger than the legendary Satchel Paige's. In fact, several Major League players who had faced both black players and the owner of the Negro Leagues' Cuban Stars saw a brighter future for Wright than Robinson. "John had all the ability in the world," Robinson asserted. "[B]ut I feel he didn't have the right kind of temperament to make it [in white baseball] in those days. He couldn't withstand the pressure of taking insult after insult without being able to retaliate. It affected his pitching that he had to keep his temper under control all the time." Monte Irvin, a prominent Negro Leaguer who broke into the Major Leagues in 1949, also heralded Wright's talent, but believed "being around white people would sometimes scare him, and he never did overcome it."

Wright's playing position likely made a difference as well. Certainly walking onto a field surrounded by racist whites required tremendous courage, but arguably no defensive position on a baseball diamond comes with more pressure and isolation than the man who stands atop the pitcher's mound. Now it is simply the African American hurler against the white batter; heaven forbid his command of the inside pitch slip to hit the man at the plate. "His margin of error was small," notes one baseball historian. "Suddenly, you're not pitching. You're aiming."

One essential difference between Wright and Robinson might further explain the former's understandable anxiety. "I am a Southerner," Wright reminded. "I have always lived in the South, so I know what is coming." The product of a New Orleans housing project, Wright's Jim Crow experiences surely had given him ample reason for caution and concern about the difficulties inherent in this interracial experiment. Robinson, of course, had grown up in the comparably less oppressive environment of California, and perhaps, thankfully, he did not know what he didn't know about the depths of white supremacist determination. While he would sadly be much better educated on the subject in the coming years, he entered the Dodgers without already being as worn by the full suffocating, grinding encounters to which Wright must have been subjected.

Whatever the causes, Wright's early struggles no doubt contributed to his demotion very early in the regular season. Rickey immediately signed another Negro League pitcher, Roy Partlow, to replace Wright at the Royals. Like Wright, Partlow was a highly regarded pitcher, recording the most strikeouts in the Negro National League in 1945. Partlow lasted only two months, and he joined Wright at the Class C Three Rivers squad. Partlow performed admirably there for the remainder of the season, a major contributor to the team, which won the league championship. He would be invited, along with Robinson, to next season's Dodgers spring training; he failed to make the team and returned to the Negro Leagues before retiring a few years later.

As for Wright, he continued to pitch inconsistently for Three Rivers during the 1946 season, still displaying signs of great talent, including winning the deciding game of the championship series. "I would just like to get another shot at Montreal," he told the press after the win. He never got it. Wright was released in January, played two more years in the Negro Leagues, and a couple in the Mexican Leagues before leaving baseball for good. (While he never said so publicly, one can't help but believe that he found in Mexico what he couldn't in his native land—far less racist treatment.) Negro League teammate Wilmer Fields perceptively noted, "John never talked much about his experience with the Dodgers. He was a happy-go-lucky person who was in the wrong place at the wrong time."

Wright returned to New Orleans to work quietly in a gypsum plant for the remainder of his years, eschewing interviews. "He didn't ever, ever, ever talk about it with anybody I knew," recalled one of the few coworkers who was privy to Wright's historic role. "He was . . . close-lipped about it. If you didn't ask the right question, you didn't get the answer." Walter Wright (no relation), president of the local black old-timers players association, delivered the eulogy at Johnny's 1990 funeral. "[H]e died with a volume of information that he never released to anyone. You never knew how he felt." Recalling that funeral several years later, he lamented, "[W]hen I looked over at his casket, I couldn't help wondering how many stories it contained—stories that now would never be told."

CHAPTER FIVE

The Great Experiment

Robinson Ascends to the Major Leagues

Following Robinson's highly successful run with the Montreal Royals in 1946, expectations mounted that it was time for his advancement to the Dodgers. The difficulties of preparing Robinson's white Dodger teammates for his arrival was still to come. In early February, Rickey approached local black leaders with a controversial speech delivered at the Brooklyn YMCA. The invite list included virtually all significant African Americans in the New York area: from doctors to lawyers, morticians, architects, and a judge. Rickey was one of only four white attendees in the sizeable and distinguished group. After the dinner plates were cleared, Rickey launched into a lengthy, unscripted, frank speech. In surprising language, he warned black leaders that the "biggest threat" to the probable ensuing experiment of a black player in the Major Leagues was not white resistance, but "the Negro people themselves." In words that would strike a contemporary as shockingly patronizing and tone deaf, Rickey chastened that "[e]very one of you will go out and form parades and welcoming committees. You'll strut. You'll wear badges. . . . You'll get drunk. You'll fight. You'll be arrested. You'll wine and dine the player until he is fat and futile." Then, to an assembly of men who had lived their lives under white supremacy, he warned, "If any individual, group or segment of Negro society" painted Robinson's rise "as a symbol of social 'ism' or schism, a triumph of race over race, I will curse the day I signed him to a contract." It would be up to this noble black middle class, Rickey cautioned, to ensure the lesser black citizens did not end up "spoiling Jackie's chances."

The black leaders present, eager no doubt to see any racial advancement, responded to Rickey's jeremiad by organizing a "Master Committee." It would carry out Rickey's wishes to tamp down the unsophisticated overexuberance of the black working class—which could in turn arouse a backlash among the white masses. New black migrants from the rural South were especially the targets of these concerns. The committee then spread the word in a variety of ways—through the pulpit, in newspaper editorials, social gatherings, and fraternal lodges. Such committees even did similar work in National League cities where Robinson might appear.

Confident that another potential problem had been averted, Rickey proceeded with his carefully planned spring training, determined that it be "perfectly smooth." A central feature of that plan was leaving the United States. The Dodgers would hold camp in 1947 in Cuba and play several additional games in Panama, hoping to shelter Robinson from the distractions of American racism beyond the playing fields. But even in Cuba, Rickey felt forced to make concessions to racial animus. While the white Dodgers stayed at the swank Havana Hotel Nacional overlooking the Caribbean, the Robinsons were forced to reside at a downtown "musty third-rate hotel." Rickey sought to avoid a "possible racial incident" should a black player presume to check in at the Nacional, and the "indignant" Robinson "reluctantly accepted" Rickey's explanation. Amid it all, Rickey continued to insist to Robinson, "I want you to win the friendship of people everywhere. You must be personable, you must smile, and even if they are worrying you to death, make the public think you don't mind."

Enduring it with him were the soon-to-be-dismissed Roy Partlow and two other black players, Roy Campanella and Don Newcombe. The latter two men had entered white baseball with considerably less fanfare than Robinson at the Class B Nashua team in the New England League, but were part of Rickey's wider plan to integrate his organization. Campanella was the product of an Italian American father and African American mother. Like Robinson, his Philadelphia youth included integrated education and sports teams. So talented was he that he began professional play as a weekend-only contestant at the ripe age of sixteen in the Negro Leagues. Leaving school at two o'clock on Friday afternoons to make the night game with the Baltimore Elite Giants, he competed in the Saturday and Sunday games before returning to his high school classes on Monday morning. Hence, at the age of twenty-five, the hard-hitting catcher was already a nine-year professional veteran. The nineteen-year-old Newcombe was still growing into his six-foot-four frame, but he had already shown enough promise for Rickey to see a bright future. Together, they helped lead Nashua to win their league's 1946 pen-nant. Campanella had even been named the league's Most Valuable Player that year. Now they were getting their chance on the Major League level.

The substandard African American accommodations hampered far more than the four black players' pride and dignity. The white players' resort hotel catered to an American clientele; the staff at the black players' shoddy hotel spoke no English. Campanella had a limited knowledge of Spanish, and when he was unavailable, his three black cohorts were essentially helpless. More troubling was the available diet. Stranded in the poorer section of Havana, the African American athletes were left with a steady stream of fried foods with extremely suspect sanitary conditions. Newcombe recalled greeting a cockroach in his soup in one establishment. So severe did the problem become that Robinson found his stomach health "hanging on the ropes" as he suffered from dysentery and, later, an inflamed colon in the midst of taking on the tremendous physical challenge of making the roster.

Had Robinson known what was happening behind the scenes among the white players, his stomach would have been in a worse state. A petition circulated among the white Dodgers opposing any black teammates. Fan favorite Dixie Walker was said to be its author. It had apparently gained special traction among the several southern players.

A typically determined Leo Durocher, the team's field manager, would have none of it. He called a 2 a.m. meeting in the hotel kitchen clothed in a yellow bathrobe and plenty of expletives: "I don't care if a guy is yellow or black, or if he has stripes like a f***ing zebra. I'm the manager of this team and I say he plays." To leave no doubt, he recommended any player's best use of the petition would be to "wipe [his] ass with it." Rickey had promised to trade any player who harbored uncertainty over the matter (and later did so with two of the signatories). With that, the controversy died down. Though Durocher's often fiery demeanor was especially helpful in this instance, Dodgers' road secretary Harold Parrott couldn't help but note the irony of Leo Durocher confronting the team on a racial issue: he "wouldn't have been able to spell equality much less preach it. He would have been the first to tell you that all men were not created equal."

Robinson faced an additional challenge on the baseball diamond: playing the new position of first base. So unprepared was he for the change, he took the position wearing a clubhouse custodian's first baseman's glove (who was duly compensated $15). It was so uncomfortable a fit that even when asked if the mitt was a proper match, he responded, "I honestly wouldn't know. I never had one on before." Comfortable or not, first base is where the Dodgers had an opening, and, with time, both Robinson's bat and glove began to prove his worth.

Just as Rickey prepared himself for the dawning of his racial experiment on a baseball diamond, a body blow came from the commissioner's office. Following a series of controversial episodes, Leo Durocher was now suspended for a year for "conduct detrimental to baseball." Durocher had always been a colorful figure, cavorting with Hollywood's beautiful people, taking up with a film starlet whose divorce had not been finalized, and associating with gamblers. While those activities had often unnerved his strict Sabbath-observing "Deacon" of an employer, Rickey had an unshakeable fondness for his field manager—born both from Rickey's missionary zeal that he could lead the man to the straight and narrow and the intensity for winning baseball that both men shared. Now the matter was out of Rickey's hands, and he refused to have the absence of a pilot run his ready ship aground. A week later, he reached for an unlikely solution: his old friend Burt Shotton.

Shotton had worked for Rickey both as a player (during Rickey's stint as a manager of the St. Louis Browns) and as a Minor League manager in Rickey's St. Louis Cardinals farm system. He went on to distinguish himself as a manager of other Minor and Major League teams. Shotton finally retired in 1945, pledging never to don a uniform again. He had subsequently agreed to a part-time Dodgers scouting position. And so it was that his once-again employer Branch Rickey sent a most mercurial telegram to his Florida retreat: "Be in Brooklyn tomorrow morning. See nobody. Say nothing. Rickey." A dutiful Shotton did just that, expecting that the Mahatma merely "wants to see me about some players," as he told his wife.

After a long breakfast and leisurely conversation over trivia at the New York airport, Rickey took Shotton on a pleasant drive into Manhattan. He then pulled the car to the curb and announced two things: that he was now getting a haircut, and "Burt, you know the way to the Polo Grounds. I want you to manage the Dodgers. Good luck." Thus did Shotton find himself in the dugout that afternoon, the newly installed skipper without a change of clothes. Nor would the eccentric Shotton change into the traditional on-field uniform during the season. He would stand quietly at the end of the bench in a Dodgers cap and jacket and his shirt and tie—some said in order to keep his promise to his wife to never wear a baseball uniform again. He was a bookish, unassuming, bow-tie-clad stalwart counterpoint to the pugnacious, street smart, emotional firebrand of his predecessor. And in the choppy waters that lay ahead in the 1947 season, perhaps what the team ironically needed was a steady, quiet hand at the wheel.

There were more immediate concerns for Jackie Robinson, and just five days before the Dodgers began their regular season campaign, his waiting finally came to an end when he signed a contract to join a Major League team. An unsurprisingly ecstatic Robinson now would pay closer attention "whenever I hear my wife read fairy tales to my little boy . . . I know now that dreams do come true." Those sentiments were echoed in the black press—the *Boston Chronicle* featured the headline, "Triumph of Whole Race Seen in Jackie's Debut in Major League Ball." Even his ensuing game time dugout seating arrangements did not escape scrutiny by African American journalists, including an account of pitcher Vic Lombardi who "started to take the next seat [beside Robinson], changed his mind and wedged in between two other players."

More surprising was how relatively straightforward the first week of Robinson's 1947 season seemed, especially as the white press handled baseball's integration far more quietly, often limiting any news on Robinson to the confines of daily game reports. Some reported an undeniable buzz in the air when play centered on Robinson, but after a year of drama and hype, one white sportswriter claimed the merely two-thirds-capacity Brooklyn opening-day crowd "took the event in stride." By the weekend, Robinson packed the crosstown Polo Grounds stadium in Harlem for a visiting game against the New York Giants. While performing well, coverage of Robinson was overshadowed in the mainline newspapers by the recent hiring of Shotton as manager.

It was a week into the season that the inevitable racial confrontations emerged on the field in the person of Ben Chapman. Chapman had brought both his Philadelphia Phillies and his deep-seated racism to Ebbets Field in late April. Certainly taunting opposing batters from the dugout had long been a regular, if not a bit sophomoric, part of America's game, but manager Ben Chapman twisted the tradition into what most observers saw as a virulent, distasteful direction. "They're waiting for you in the jungles, black boy!" he jeered. Peppering many of the catcalls with "nigger," he also loudly demanded, "Which one of those white boys' wives are you dating tonight?" What's more, Chapman was joined by many of his players, who had been reportedly ordered to aid him in the epithets, including a warning to the white Dodgers about their certain infection from unusual diseases and maladies should they come into contact with Robinson's personal effects. So bad was it that disturbed fans wrote the commissioner of baseball to complain (which did cause him to demand the harassment end), and notable news journalist Walter Winchell took a portion of his national Sunday night radio broadcast to castigate Chapman.

As for Robinson, his pledge to refrain from retaliation might have ended a week into his first season right then and there. The abusive spilling of epithets "brought me nearer to cracking up" than he had ever been in his life. What "did Mr. Rickey expect of me?" he asked himself. "I was after all, a human being." And ever more so in the social climate of the 1940s, withholding his anger ate at the core of his masculinity. "What was I doing here turning the other cheek as though I weren't a man?" In a later account, he recalled his reputation for a quick temper in his younger years, noting, "In college days I had had a reputation as a black man who never tolerated affronts to his dignity. I had defied prejudice in the Army." Then came the "one wild and rage-crazed minute" that almost cost his pledge to Rickey.

> I thought, "To hell with Mr. Rickey's 'noble experiment.' . . . I thought what a glorious, cleansing thing it would be to let go. To hell with the image of the patient black freak I was supposed to create. I could throw down my bat, stride over to that Phillies dugout, grab one of those white sons of bitches and smash his teeth in with my despised black fist."

Famously, however, Robinson simply swallowed hard and brought his curled black fist back to the home dugout. While Robinson scored the winning run in the first game of the Phillies' series, the bitter taste of this incident lingered as the abuse appeared to affect his play in the last two games—which began a batting drought. A minor encouraging sign emerged by the series' second game, when Robinson's white teammates finally began to defend him, calling Chapman a "coward" who should "pick on somebody who can fight back."

Despite Chapman's efforts to defend his actions as nothing more than routine attempts to unsettle an opposing player, public pressure continued to mount against him. The Dodgers' visiting series in Philadelphia a few weeks later brought an unwelcome postscript to the episode for Robinson. Both team owners encouraged a conciliatory photo be taken of Chapman and Robinson shaking hands on the dugout steps. Robinson could "think of no occasion where I had more difficulty in swallowing my pride" and staying true to his commitment "than in agreeing to pose for that photograph with a man for whom I had only the very lowest regard. But I did it, although deep in my heart I could not forgive Chapman and the Phillies for what they had tried to do."

As they posed for the press, Chapman—for whom Robinson was doing a favor to aid his besmirched reputation—had the audacity to mumble audibly enough for a few Phillies players to hear, "Jackie, you're a good ballplayer, but you're still a nigger to me." True to the cause, Robinson nevertheless publicly stated at the time to being "glad" to take the photo with someone who "impressed me as a nice fellow," adding that "I don't really think he meant the things he was shouting at me." The peace was short-lived, as the Phillies quickly picked up the racist heckling where they had left it, albeit in an admittedly muted fashion—including players who "pointed bats at me and made machine-gunlike noises."

The latter was especially unnerving given the death threats that were arriving in the Robinsons' mailbox. Hate mail came in consistently, but some correspondence was more specific: kidnapping threats against his wife and baby, and assassination warnings to him and his family. As such letters grew in frequency, the Dodgers' front office decided to screen his mail in order to shield Robinson from the worry. Some were deemed serious enough to turn over to police, who assigned a secret squad to investigate, but the authors could not be located. An especially unsettling cluster targeted a Dodgers series in Cincinnati. Club official Harold Parrott felt these were so specific that he must overlook his usual penchant to withhold them from Robinson, and he "could see that [Robinson] was frightened" as the trip approached. The FBI, in fact, searched the rooftops and upper floors of nearby buildings. When the park's playing of the national anthem's crescendo included the recorded sounds of explosions, it alarmed Parrott that this "would have been the ideal cover for gunfire." It would not be the only time that it must have occurred to Robinson that standing alone at first base surrounded by thousands of strangers with unknown motivations made him an ideal sniper target. It was a thought that certainly hadn't escaped his wife's mind, who would find herself worrying in darker moments about "some crazy or irrational person who might shoot from the stands." Rachel found it very difficult to get her husband to speak of his challenges since "he didn't want to burden me. . . . But I knew they were eating at his mind, for he would jerk and twitch and even talk in his troubled sleep."

The white Dodgers players' interactions with their black infielder were another troubling matter. Things appeared to go largely smoothly on the field, but in the clubhouse "I would know the strain and pressure of being a stranger." While traveling, Robinson would often pair up with a black sportswriter. When one wasn't along, he simply "sat by myself while the other guys chatted and laughed and played cards." Jackie often took his meals alone, so as not to force white teammates into the uncomfortably unfamiliar situation of sharing a table with an African American. Gradually, their relations relaxed, although not entirely in many cases. As they did, interactions could sometimes produce revealing and unsettling honesties. Relief pitcher Hugh Casey, who had been one of the more supportive white players, sought to make light of his poor stakes during one of the rare poker games in which Robinson had been invited. An inebriated Casey leaned over the table to rub Robinson's head, asking whether he knew "what I used to do down in Georgia when I ran into bad luck? I used to go out and find me the biggest, blackest nigger woman I could find and rub her teats to change my luck." Even Casey's fellow white cohorts were stunned into a "horrified silence." Swallowing his anger yet again by reminding himself of "Mr. Rickey's words . . . I made myself turn to the dealer and told him to deal the cards."

Exacerbating Robinson's isolation were hotel restrictions in St. Louis, Philadelphia, and Cincinnati. Brooklyn officials made the decision not to challenge segregation customs, so their lone black player stayed in separate Negro hotels in the former two cities. Arrangements were made to allow Robinson to reside in the Cincinnati location on the provision that he eat only in his room to avoid upsetting white customers in the hotel restaurant. As these collective pressures mounted in the early weeks of May, Robinson's psyche and batting average appeared to sag (the latter to a pedestrian .250). One sportswriter saw the Dodgers first baseman as "the loneliest man I have ever seen in sports." Robinson later recounted "feeling like a black Don Quixote tilting at a lot of white windmills."

By the last half of May, though, Robinson's impact and excellence were apparent. His team's appearance brought out the largest crowd in Chicago's storied Wrigley Field and the season's most sizeable weekday attendance in St. Louis. While his numbers would all increase as the season revved up, many observers began to realize that Robinson's impact went well beyond the simple statistical sheet. "Never have records meant so little in discussing a player's value," claimed sportswriter Tom Meany. His very "presence" lit "a fire under his own team and unsettle[d] his opponents." Fellow sports scribe John Crosby saw Robinson as "the greatest opportunist on any kind of playing field, seeing openings before they opened, pulling off plays lesser players can't even imagine." This unpredictable opportunism, which—in the words of historian Jules Tygiel—"revolutionized major league baseball" after his arrival, may have been surprising to his white competitors, but it had long been the norm in the Negro Leagues he had now left behind. Staples of black baseball he now used included his virtually constant inclination to threaten stealing base and his frequent bunting (in part because simply getting on base opened the possibility of progressing much further through stealing). Teammate Rex Barney remembers Robinson as "the most exciting player I have ever seen. . . . As long as he was in the game, you had a chance to win. The second he got on base, the whole ballpark, you could feel them get on the edge of their seats. They knew he was going to do something."

More than that, the danger of Robinson's base stealing unsettled his opponents so significantly that his mere presence on the base paths made teammates' plays possible. *Time* magazine reported that he "dances and prances off base, keeping the enemy infield upset and off balance, and worrying the pitcher." Yankees hurler Vic Raschi remembers how the Dodger great shattered "my concentration" in the 1949 World Series until "I was pitching more to [hold] Robinson [at first base] than I was to [batter Gil] Hodges," causing him to throw "one up into Gil's power and he got the base hit to beat me." Similarly, pitcher Gene Conley recalled a famous game-winner crushed by Carl Furillo. "Furillo got all the headlines, but I knew it was Robinson who had distracted me just enough to hang that curve."

By June, recognition of Robinson's contributions was near universal. By the end of the month, he had built an impressive .315 batting average, a

Figure 5.1.   Robinson shares a moment with teammate Pee Wee Reese in the Brooklyn Dodgers' dugout. *Source*: **Library of Congress, http://www.loc.gov/pictures/item/ 2008679074/**

league lead in stolen bases, and a rank of second in runs scored. His sterling play was a crucial reason that the Dodgers occupied first place in the National League race in July. Despite the many racial challenges he faced, Robinson's insurmountable competitive drive was winning out. Hall of Fame teammate Duke Snider remembers observing him "get into uniform. Jack would joke and kid and talk about the racetrack. But as he pulled on the Brooklyn shirt and the blue Brooklyn stirrups and the Brooklyn pants and the blue Brooklyn cap, he just got more and more serious. He was putting on his game face. Jack had a helluva game face: Take no prisoners."

By midsummer, the Cleveland Indians joined the ranks of integrated baseball by making Negro League player Larry Doby the first African American player in the American League. Robinson congratulated the "grand guy and . . . very good ball player. I'm glad to know that another Negro player is in the majors. I'm no longer in there by myself." The St. Louis Browns soon added three Negro Leaguers to their once all-white club as well. The Browns' additions faced a decidedly hostile reception among their white counterparts and were gone by August. Doby proved to be a success after a slow first season, and would later earn a place in the Hall of Fame.

Branch Rickey, too, grew eager in August for more black talent to bolster his pitching staff. He traveled personally to Memphis to see the Negro League Red Sox hurler Dan Bankhead strike out eleven batters. Suitably impressed, Rickey bought his contract and had Bankhead join the Dodgers two days later. Hence, Bankhead got none of the Minor League seasoning other black Dodger signees had enjoyed; though Rickey would have preferred that, pitching help was needed too urgently. Bankhead made four difficult appearances before being relegated to the Minors. (After working his way back to Brooklyn in 1950, he was released again for good by 1951.) Dodger publicist Irving Rudd claimed the fast-throwing Bankhead could have been "one of the greatest pitchers in baseball history if he were white," but he had been "emotionally scarred by racism" and was unable to rise to the considerable challenges that had confronted Robinson.

As season's end approached, the St. Louis Cardinals came charging from behind at the Dodgers' league lead. That brought intense focus to a mid-August series between the two in Brooklyn. The teams split the four-game series, but far more attention was given to two infield plays. In the first game, Cardinals batter Joe Medwick drove his cleat spikes into Robinson's foot as he ran to claim first base, drawing blood, but most observers saw no ill intent. Medwick's play, however, no doubt lingered on Dodgers' minds as they viewed Cardinal Enos Slaughter for the final game of the series. Running out the baseline, Slaughter—who had been rumored to be the instigator for an aborted player strike against Robinson early in the season—landed his spikes high on Robinson's left leg, barely missing his Achilles tendon. Dodgers announcer Red Barber claimed that the black infielder's career thus "came within an inch of being ended." Several enraged Dodgers teammates threatened "dire consequences" if Robinson were roughed up further, but Slaughter denied any willful harm. Jackie, pulling up at first base after singling in his next at-bat, told the future Hall of Fame opposing first baseman, Stan Musial, "I don't care what happens, but when I get to second base, I'm gonna kill somebody. I'm gonna knock him into center field." Even Musial confided to his opponent, "You have every right to do it." Yet again, however, Robinson swallowed his rage and took second without incident.

A month later, hostilities were renewed in St. Louis as the Cardinals still sought four-and-one-half games to claim the National League championship from the Dodgers. When Cardinal catcher Joe Garagiola spiked Robinson's heel at first base, it "cut my shoe all to pieces," he told the press following the game. With the earlier series histrionics brought back to mind, Robinson confronted Garagiola in the subsequent inning as he came to bat. He appeared to be on or over the line of his commitment to Rickey as he "engaged in an angry teeth-to-teeth exchange" with the Cardinal catcher, according to one reporter. The argument was brought on by a remark Robinson seemed to make first to Garagiola, followed by a possible racist response (which Robinson claims was made and Garagiola denied). The umpire interceded as both men moved aggressively toward one another, appearing to be on the verge of a fistfight. A Brooklyn coach, racing onto the field, finally ended the showdown by restraining his player. It is an incident that has dogged Garagiola throughout his distinguished baseball and popular television career and beyond. "Jackie was a firebrand," he told a recent interviewer, "Even in '47 he was a competitor. You're fighting for the pennant, and who cares what color he is. . . . He said something to me. I said, 'Why don't you just hit' . . . I've lived with this thing unfairly. It was a little bit of jockeying to break his concentration, that's all. . . . It wasn't even an argument. . . . You just don't know the grief and aggravation this has caused."

Directing his anger at a fastball, Robinson homered in the next inning, and went on to play both exceptionally at the plate and in the field, helping his team to win the series and keep the pennant firmly out of the Cardinals' clutches. *Time* magazine, which put Jackie Robinson on a September cover, wrote that much of that championship could be credited to their African American recruit. The *Sporting News*—once skeptical of the advisability of

Robinson's inclusion—gave him their prestigious Rookie of the Year Award. And southerner Dixie Walker, said to have led the anti-Robinson petition in training camp, now sung his black teammate's praises: "No other ball-player on this club, with the possible exception of [catcher] Bruce Edwards has done more to put the Dodgers up in the race than Robinson has." In late September, Dodgers home stadium hosted "Jackie Robinson Day," including many gifts, civic officials' praise, and an appearance by acclaimed black entertainer Bill "Bojangles" Robinson, who named Jackie "Ty Cobb in Technicolor."

What followed was one of the most exciting World Series in baseball history. Crosstown rivals New York Yankees emerged as the opponent, considerably heightening the stakes. The Dodgers drove the series to a full seven games before succumbing to the Yankees' superior pitching. Robinson played well, but not quite up to his late-season extraordinary standards.

Still, there was no getting around his massive impact on his team, on the game, even on American society. By late 1947, Americans named the black infielder the astonishing second most popular man in the country. He was widely celebrated for his courage, humility, sportsmanship, and for being a fine family man. President Harry Truman's own civil rights committee (appointed to examine the racial tensions emerging in postwar America) issued a largely pessimistic report and called for a number of reforms in 1947. One of the events in which it found reason for optimism was the integration of the Dodgers.

But Robinson's impact scattered into millions of powerful individual stories as well that never made headlines. Roger Wilkins, later to become an assistant U.S. Attorney General and a Pulitzer Prize–winning journalist, was a fifteen-year-old black boy in Michigan when Robinson broke into white baseball. Wilkins remembers him "as important to me and other blacks, especially young blacks, as a parent would have been, I think. Because he brought pride and the certain knowledge that on a fair playing field, when there were rules and whites could not cheat and lie and steal, not only were they not supermen but we could beat 'em. . . . And this man, in a very personal sense, became a permanent part of my spirit and the spirit of a generation of black kids." Noted black journalist Sam Lacy remembers Robinson's influence extending well beyond the baselines of a ballpark as well: "No matter what the nature of the gathering, a horse race, a church meeting, a ball game, the universal question is: 'How'd Jackie make out today?'" Mike Royko, later to be a famous white columnist, was just a boy when he attended

Figure 5.2. Robinson's impact, of course, extended far beyond the field of play, as evidenced by this young boy holding a copy of "Negro Heroes" magazine with Jackie on the cover. *Source*: Library of Congress, http://www.loc.gov/pictures/item/2003688484/

Robinson's first game in his native Chicago. As a grown man, he recalled how Jackie not only integrated Wrigley Field but briefly and surprisingly the city's population as well. "Few blacks were seen in downtown Chicago, much less up on the white North side at a Cub game. That day they came by the thousands, pouring off the north-bound ELS and out of their cars." They obviously left an impression on white Chicagoans. "They didn't wear baseball-game clothes," he remembers. "They had on church clothes. . . . The whites tried to look as if nothing unusual was happening, while the blacks tried to look casual and dignified. So everybody looked ill at ease. For the most part it was probably the first time they had been so close to each other in such large numbers." They would be back, of course, in coming years to demand more than a baseball ticket.

With the "great experiment" safely behind him, Robinson now sought to bring his family some economic security. In the late 1940s, $5,000 was an enviable salary for an African American, but it was also the league minimum, and he was well aware that sports careers did not last long in the best of circumstances. Offers were plentiful, and he accepted many—from endorsing Homogenized Bond bread to Old Gold cigarettes. He signed a contract to appear in a film of his story (which would never be made), and to allow friend and sportswriter Wendell Smith to write a book about his story. He even spent four weeks traveling with a vaudeville show. Reviews of the latter were hardly favorable, and some questioned if his appearance in a poorly run black vaudeville troupe undermined the public image of black dignity he had bolstered in the preceding baseball season. "Everything Jackie had worked so hard to build, giving us an intelligent and capable ball player, was crumbled among those degrading surroundings," said a reviewer. Such criticism, though, only amplified the special burden for his race that he found himself carrying and the limited career opportunities for black males in postwar America. Surely he would have preferred a Wall Street position to vaudeville. This tension between outside expectations and actual opportunity to provide for himself and his family would remain an issue in his postbaseball years.

The 1948 Dodgers spring training began in Ciudad Trujillo, Dominican Republic, in early March. For the second consecutive year, Rickey chose a foreign location to avoid the probable racist distractions of the commonly used southern United States. Having spent much of the offseason touring the banquet circuit, Robinson arrived with a myriad of bestowed honors and an unwelcome extra twenty-five to thirty pounds. Newly reinstated field manager Leo Durocher—fresh off his league suspension—was not pleased.

At first sighting of his mildly rotund black infielder, and in full view of sportswriters, Durocher exclaimed that Jackie looked "like an old woman . . . [with] all that fat around your midsection." Under his manager's orders, Robinson spent much of his month in the Caribbean fielding extra ground balls in a rubber suit (to induce weight loss) in front of the other players, with Durocher shouting, "Stick a fork in him, he's done. C'mon fatso, get moving!" Publicly Jackie expressed support and understanding for the skipper's tactics, but some writers began to report "bad blood" between the two.

As the team headed back to America to begin the season, their plane lost an engine. In an unnerving sequence, another engine began misfiring, and the pilot swiftly turned the craft back, finally touching down to safety. "Sure we were scared," conceded Robinson. While another airliner took them to Florida for an exhibition series, the shaky journey could serve as a metaphor for the 1948 Dodger season. Rickey first unsettled Brooklyn fans by trading two popular players: Eddie Stanky and Dixie Walker. The gritty Stanky had made the cardinal error of asking for additional money from the notoriously skinflint Rickey; moving him also opened up second base, now deemed a more natural position for Robinson. While Walker was very talented, he had grown long in the tooth, prone to injury, and overpaid. The trade also put closure to the troubled beginning of Robinson's ascension to the Majors. Walker had been suspected of spearheading the Dodger players' anti-Robinson petition a year prior, which had certainly not endeared him to the Mahatma. Nevertheless, the always complicated Rickey could have traded Walker immediately after the petition had surfaced, but he apparently needed his bat too badly; he had also offered Walker the option of retiring to a Dodgers farm club managerial role before the trade—something Walker declined in favor of playing two more years. Years later, Walker remembered Robinson as "a stemwinder of a ballplayer. But, you know, we never hit it off real well." Maintaining that he'd "gotten along with a lot of blacks since then," he regarded Robinson "as a very antagonistic person. . . . Maybe he had to be to survive. The curses, the threats on his life. I don't know if I could have gone through what he did."

Robinson's weight problem continued to linger into the regular season, despite losing most of the excess in spring training. His slower gait was evident to the naked eye and on the stat sheet (where he was without a stolen base in the season's first two months). Rickey even called his performance "sluggish." Sadly, that merely mirrored the whole team's lumbering performance as it stumbled out of the gate in 1948. When a six-game losing skid brought them to last place at midseason, Rickey had finally seen enough.

Looking for a smooth way out of directly firing his longtime employee, Rickey suggested Durocher take the recently opened field manager job with the crosstown rival New York Giants.

With a new vacancy in his clubhouse, Rickey once again called his old friend Burt Shotton out of retirement. Robinson, whose friction with Durocher had become apparent to observers, was elated. "I love playing for Shotton. . . . When Shotton wants to bawl out a player he takes him aside and does it in private. . . . If Leo has something on his mind, you hear it right there—but loud, and in front of everyone who's around." The trait certainly sat poorly with a player already enduring excessive public scrutiny.

One bone of contention between Rickey and his manager had been Roy Campanella, who enjoyed a brief stint with the Dodgers in April and May before being sent back to the St. Paul farm club on Rickey's insistence. Durocher felt rightly that Campanella was badly needed as the organization's best catcher, but Rickey still retained misguided faith in their 1947 catcher Bruce Edwards and wanted the distinction of integrating the American Association Minor League (to which St. Paul belonged). When Campanella finally ascended to Brooklyn for good in July, he quickly became the regular catcher and contributed to a notable late-season Dodger surge (with Durocher, of course, not there to reap the reward). Robinson likewise turned his season around, becoming the team's leader in batting average, runs batted in, and runs scored. He was named the league's best fielding second baseman as well.

It was not enough. The Dodgers, who had occupied last place at midseason, were only able to climb into third before the season concluded. Still, Rickey took solace in the young talent the team was building for the future and in the racial progress that continued. Brooklyn now had two very strong African American stars of the future on their roster, and more on the way in the Minors.

Also satisfying was the path of the Cleveland Indians. Larry Doby remained a reliable black starter, and they joined the Dodgers in having two African Americans on their roster in July. In the heat of a pennant race in the summer of 1948, colorful Cleveland Indians owner Bill Veeck did what he had toyed with doing for years: he signed legendary pitcher Satchel Paige. Having watched him pitch a thirteen-inning shutout over the white master of the mound, Dizzy Dean, in 1934 California, Veeck had long dreamed of putting Paige on his payroll. Fearing both the lanky hurler's age and less-than-choirboy reputation, Veeck had veered from hiring Paige as his first choice over Larry Doby a year earlier. Needing to bolster his pitching staff now for a late-season run, however, the temptation was too great; and, at age forty-two, Paige became the oldest rookie in Major League history. Gone, of course, were Paige's best years while white clubs had dawdled over the question of race. Sports fans had been cheated out of the possible memories of the lanky hurler delivering his famous stare to the best white players for two decades. However sluggish in arriving, he finally got his shot.

Far less could be said of Josh Gibson. Like Jackie Robinson, Josh Gibson was born in Georgia, and then taken from the Jim Crow South as a youngster in the 1920s for better racial and economic climes. "The greatest gift Dad gave me," Gibson later opined, "was to get me out of the South." It did not take long for observers to note the young Gibson's prodigious baseball talent, which he first plied professionally with the Homestead Grays in 1930. Later moving across town to the rival Negro League team, the Pittsburgh Crawfords, in 1932, Gibson helped form the nucleus of a legendary team—"the Yankees of Negro baseball," as Major League pitching great Bob Feller called them—with pitching giant Satchel Paige and sluggers Buck Leonard, Sam Bankhead, and Vic Harris. While accurate records on the Negro Leagues were rarely kept, it seems clear that Gibson was every bit the equal—if not the superior—of his white power-hitting counterpart of the era, Babe Ruth. "If you wanted to see a man who looked like trouble at the bat," recalled a competitor, "look at Josh." So great was his talent that the fanciful stories that followed Gibson almost seemed true. One recounted Gibson's crush of a pitch went so far and high that no observer saw it come down. After searching the clouds for several minutes, an umpire was forced to declare it a homer. But when a ball fell inexplicably from the heavens during the next day's game, the official declared Gibson out—yesterday.

By 1939, Gibson's fame brought attention beyond the color line. *Washington Post* writer Shirley Povich claimed that Gibson was superior to Yankee great (and future Hall of Famer) Bill Dickey. Former Washington Senator Walter Johnson, one of the first men elected to the Baseball Hall of Fame and the holder of numerous pitching records, alerted the public of "a catcher that any big league club would like to buy. . . . His name is Gibson . . . he can do everything. He hits the ball a mile. And he catches so easy he might as well be in a rocking chair. Throws like a rifle. . . . Too bad this Gibson is a colored fellow." As the attention grew, rumors spread that the Pittsburgh Pirates (a Major League team) were scheduling a tryout for Gibson with the intent to sign him. It never occurred, reportedly due to the Pirates owner's last-minute cold feet. The great black catcher simply returned to the Homestead Grays, biding his time to bring his mighty bat to the big leagues. He and other Negro League greats would have to hope and wait that the Dodgers "experiment" would open the turnstiles for other black players.

The rumors that Gibson would get his chance at the Majors had circulated since 1939 but never materialized. He could only stand and watch as another player made it to the big leagues in his stead. African American sportswriter Ric Roberts remembers, "Most people don't realize what pride Josh took in being 'Mr. Black Baseball.' . . . He thought, if they're going to pick a black man, it had to be Josh Gibson. . . . How they could pick Jackie Robinson was something he never could understand. To find his kingdom in a shambles at the age of 33 was too much for him." His always heavy drinking began to escalate. There were rumors of drug use. Shortly after the Dodgers signed Robinson, police found Gibson wandering naked, and he was committed to a mental hospital.

Sadly, his health seemed to mirror the fate of black baseball. Just as the Negro League rosters were soon to be depleted by white teams, so, too, his once strong and healthy frame began to shrink away—from a playing weight of 220 pounds down to 180 ("just a shell of a man," said one friend). The heavy drinking, chronic hypertension, and ailing knees were finally catching up to him. In his last few years, he was prone to headaches, dizzy spells, bouts of depression, and more trips to sanitariums. Despite his reduced state, the once mighty slugger was so strong that he ripped off his strait jacket during one stay.

His 1947 death at the age of thirty-five remains shrouded in mystery. His family claimed that much of his behavior and health were due to a diagnosed brain tumor, for which Gibson declined treatment. Negro Leaguer Johnny Taylor has a simpler explanation: "He just drank himself to death." He claims Robinson's signing "just gnawed away at him. [Sam] Bankhead destroyed himself the same way." (The latter Negro League star became an alcoholic and could not bear even to see his brother Don pitch for the Dodgers. His death arrived in a barroom fight.) As for Satchel Paige: "I refuse to say that Josh destroyed himself. Some people say Josh Gibson died of a brain hemorrhage. I say he died of a broken heart."

His skeletal body was buried and forgotten in a numbered grave, and it took twenty-eight years before funds were raised to place a headstone. To his fellow players, however, his mark could have been far more than what was humbly etched on his belated grave slab. "The American people were denied the right to see a superstar perform," lamented one. "Had he been given the chance to participate in the American or National league, I bet he'd have hit 75 home runs a year. . . . Josh would have easily been a .400 hitter."

Some were still haunted by an incident before his death. In town to play in the nation's capital, his teammates heard strange noises, and realized they were coming from Gibson's room. As they crept closer, they saw Josh sitting by himself near his window staring off into the distance. "C'mon Joe, talk to me," said Gibson. Shaken and bewildered as to what was happening to Josh, they sat transfixed, until finally Gibson said, "Hey, Joe DiMaggio, it's me, you know me. Why don't you answer me?"

~

CHAPTER SIX

"To Be Jackie Robinson"

His Further Years in the Majors, 1949–1956

While expectations may have been modest for the 1949 Dodgers among baseball writers, Rickey entered the season with high hopes centered on a young, eager nucleus of returning players. He called it his "most promising team" since coming to Brooklyn. Robinson, too, arrived in camp that spring seemingly with more focus—and considerably less girth than the previous year. Robinson's enthusiasm stirred controversy, however, when he warned in an interview that his opponents "better be rough on me, because I'm going to be rough on them." The Major League Commissioner summoned the player to his office to explain the remarks, especially as Robinson had also threatened to punch a Minor Leaguer who pitched him inside during a spring game. Robinson reassured that his published remarks were not intended to suggest any violence, but merely hard play. Free to go, he did resent being singled out for remarks he felt would have caused barely a ripple in the press if uttered by a white player.

The kerfuffle did portend a more naturally aggressive Robinson than the public had seen in the previous three seasons. The edgier, more defiant, even angry young man that had shown up in scouting reports—and then been sublimated in his first years in white baseball—appeared to reemerge. Whether that represented a natural progression or the explicit end of the player's pledge to Rickey to "turn the other cheek" remains a matter of debate. At the time, many reporters claimed that the pledge was clearly over, and Rickey himself confirmed the idea, telling black journalist Carl Rowan, "All along I had known that the point would come when my almost-filial relationship with Jackie would break with ill feeling if I did not issue an emancipation proclamation for him. . . . So I told Robinson that he was on his own." Robinson later admitted to having "stored up a lot of hostility" during his three years of the pledge. "I had been going home nights to Rachel and young Jackie, tense and irritable, keyed up because I hadn't been able to speak out." Now, "I could fight back when I wanted." Admitting that it was "partly true" that "I wanted to get even," he noted that "more than revenge, I *wanted to be Jackie Robinson*." Teammate Rex Barney recounts Robinson telling a clubhouse meeting of Dodger veterans during spring training, "I realize there are some people here who don't like me. I don't like them any more than they like me. I know there are a lot of players in the league who have knocked me down [and] spiked me . . . and I put up with it. But I am convinced I am a major league ballplayer. . . . And from this point on, I take nothing from no one, on this team or on any other team, not from umpires or anyone else." Finally, it seems, the real Robinson that Rickey had recruited—and then sought to channel—had fully emerged.

And yet, others have denied that Rickey could really control his player in the way such an "emancipation" would suggest. Rachel Robinson claimed later in life that her husband sought no special release from Rickey—and that none was given. Instead, the perceived change in behavior simply reflected Jackie's growing comfort on the diamond and confidence that there was no going back on baseball's integration, with or without public approval of his actions. Branch Rickey's grandson claims that "Jackie was not on a leash. It was Jackie Robinson who kept Jackie Robinson from exploding. He had given a pledge he believed in and he stuck by it—that's all." In fact, there were signs that Robinson had begun to chafe against the restrictions by the end of the prior season. A number of reporters took note of Robinson's ejection from a late 1948 game for heckling an umpire as a sign of a shift in the player's on-field demeanor. Even Robinson recalled years later that the removal "made me feel great" since the official "was treating me exactly as he would any ballplayer" for the transgression.

Robinson may have started a bit slow in the 1949 season, but his batting average soon soared to second in the league by early June. Bolstering him was the arrival of a third African American player in May, pitcher Don Newcombe (Rickey had by then nine additional black players on his Minor League clubs). In July, Jackie found himself second in votes for the All-Star game, and joined by his two black teammates, Newcombe and Campanella. (Cleveland's African American pioneer, Larry Doby, also appeared.) He continued apace through the season's second half, capturing the league's batting title and Most Valuable Player award, and leading Brooklyn to the

National League championship. Newcombe also won the National League's Rookie of the Year award.

Despite these racial advancements, organized baseball still had a long way to go. There remained only seven African Americans in the Major Leagues, scattered across three teams. The everyday racist violence on the diamond also continued. "In 1949," recalled the rookie Don Newcombe, "things hadn't changed to any large degree where you could recognize it. Because they were still stepping on Jackie's foot, and they were still trying to cut Roy's chest protector off him when they slid into home plate with their spikes up in the air." The now more defiant Robinson "knew what to do when they came into second base," contended Newcombe. "Right in the mouth where you can catch them between first base in the double play. But that didn't stop pitchers from trying to hit Jackie and Roy in the head." The surging team also faced difficulties in the World Series again. When the New York Yankees swept the team and the suddenly slumping Robinson, he shrugged, "What is there to say? . . . They kicked heck out of us." Still, the 1949 season seemed to show that black players were in the big leagues to stay, and it remains Jackie's best statistical year.

More stormy weather off the field had interrupted his highly productive season when the House Un-American Activities Committee (HUAC) came calling. In 1949, the Second Red Scare was in full swing, and HUAC was one of its chief proponents. Also known as the "McCarthy Era," the Second Red Scare lasted from the late 1940s to the mid 1950s as a period of heightened alarm over the threat of communist infiltration. Fueled in part by the onset of the nuclear age, the United States also felt the rush of responsibility in being suddenly thrust into the role of only one of two superpowers— especially as its Western European democratic allies had been weakened by the recent war experience. American officials now perceived the country as the last best hope against a worldwide communist threat. These fears took flight in a four-decades-long Cold War foreign policy.

At home, the long-harbored American suspicions of leftist ideas exploded into a widely held paranoia that the United States would become a natural target of Marxists' desire to overthrow the planet's last great bastion of democractic capitalism. This "Second Red Scare" reached far and wide, from presidential executive orders to question federal government employees to interrogations of citizens' political views by congressional committees such as HUAC, state officials, local police, and private corporations. Hollywood screenwriters, political advisers, public lecturers, and community organizers among others would be scrutinized about their beliefs and organizational backgrounds or lose their livelihoods.

Amid the mounting alarm, perhaps it was no surprise that HUAC spotlighted Paul Robeson. A man with a history of questioning America, Robeson had defiantly placed himself on white conservatives' radar by asserting a comparative lack of racism in Europe, where he lived for much of the 1930s. He raised further ire by traveling to the Soviet Union and claiming that there an African American could refreshingly "walk this earth in complete dignity." Robeson was not alone in the 1930s in exploring the Communist Party of America. It earned the admiration of many African Americans during the Depression Era especially for its progressive racial policies and poverty programs amid a period of questioning the viability of capitalism. Among those who found occasional common cause with socialist and communist activists in the 1930s were NAACP cofounder and intellectual W. E. B. Du Bois, poet Langston Hughes, YWCA executive and Presidential Medal of Freedom awardee Dorothy Height, author Richard Wright, and activists Mary McLeod Bethune and Bayard Rustin. In an effort to demonstrate its full commitment to African Americans, the Party took the extraordinary step of thrice including a black organizer as its vice presidential nominee from 1932 to 1940.

Robeson wielded a remarkable range of talents. One of only three blacks at his New Jersey high school, he won the highest score on a statewide test to attend Rutgers College (at which he graduated as the lone African American). While attending Rutgers, he was twice named an All-American football player, and was named the greatest defensive end of all time by Walter Camp (largely regarded as the "Father of American football"). Like Jackie Robinson, he shone in a variety of sports, taking twelve varsity letters in four different pursuits (football, baseball, basketball, and track and field). After graduating Rutgers, he played professionally for the National Football League's first championship team before moving on to earn a law degree from Columbia University. Refused membership by the American Bar Association, he instead earned a worldwide name in singing and acting. His stage credits in Shakespeare's *Othello* (the first black actor to do so on Broadway) and two plays by the pathbreaking American Eugene O'Neill drew particular attention.

As he performed and traveled in Europe, his political awareness grew. Besides questioning American racism, he became increasingly vocal against western imperialism in Africa. To those who complained that an artist's obligation was not to offend but entertain, he remarked, "The artist must elect to fight for Freedom or for Slavery. I have made my choice. . . . The history of the era is characterized by the degradation of my people. Despoiled of their lands, their culture destroyed, they are denied equal protection of the law and deprived of their rightful place in the respect of their fellows." Robeson's calls for African independence after World War II drew increasing scrutiny as the Second Red Scare was beginning. But it was his 1949 appearance at a leftist conference for peace in Paris that became the final straw for American authorities. Chiding the United States for alleged imperialism, he went further to denounce Cold War foreign policy against a USSR that he claimed had exhibited greater progressivism on racial matters: "It is unthinkable that American Negroes would go to war on behalf of those who have oppressed us for generations against the Soviet Union which in one generation has raised our people to full human dignity." The storm of American criticism extended to African American leaders, who insisted that Robeson did not speak for the vast majority of his race. NAACP president Walter White, for example, assured white Americans that "we will not shirk our responsibilities" if a war with the Soviets arrived.

Still, Robeson's remarks tapped into long-held fears that African Americans might be insufficiently patriotic amid the high stakes of the recently onset Cold War. Hence, HUAC organized hearings allegedly to investigate concerns that African Americans' potentially weak nationalism might make them ripe ground for communist infiltration. The proceedings could also serve as a forum to spotlight Robeson's alleged disloyalty. Prominent black figures were invited in a visible display of friendly blacks' fealty to their country: from the head of the National Urban League to the Fisk University president. Heading the list would be none other than the Dodgers' second baseman.

Although Robinson would follow a parade of fellow African American witnesses to respond directly to Robeson's recent comments, interest in Robinson's appearance before HUAC stretched back a year and a half. Black committee investigator Alvin Stokes had approached Rickey and then begun negotiations with Dodgers' publicist Arthur Mann about Jackie's possible testimony. Those negotiations then continued with Robinson privately. Stokes's son has since speculated that those discussions likely included some of the player's involvements with civil rights groups that had become suspect to anticommunist crusaders. After first arriving in Brooklyn and eager to play a role in expanding racial progress beyond the Dodgers playing field, Robinson had agreed to become chair of the state committee for the United Negro and Allied Veterans of America, which strove to aid returning black vets with readjustment issues (including housing, jobs, and education). At the time, Robinson also noted his eagerness to serve under the iconic Joe Louis, who functioned as the group's "honorary national commander." He also joined the advisory board of the Solidarity Center in Harlem (a program of the International Workers Order, which provided health insurance and medical services). Both groups would later be listed as "communist front" organizations by the U.S. government. Such connections "probably caused him some trouble" that Robinson could have cleared up by his cooperation, thinks Stokes's son.

The committee's request produced considerable angst for Jackie Robinson. He recognized that he "had not yet had enough experience handling delicate problems of Negro progress to articulate for the nation the Negro's aspirations, especially when they had to be outlined against a background of political fear." But an invitation from an anticommunist government organization in 1949 fell something short of a voluntary choice. Not to participate in what Georgia congressman and committee chair John Wood termed a chance to "give the lie to statements by Paul Robeson" would cast troubling doubt on Robinson himself. Despite seeing Robeson as "an embattled and bitter man" who held a naive view of the USSR's oppressive rule, Jackie "didn't want to fall prey to the white man's game and allow myself to be pitted against another black man. I knew that Robeson was striking out against racial inequality in the way that seemed best to him." As he wavered, maddeningly differing advice "poured in" from all quarters. One highly influential voice was that of Branch Rickey, a staunch anticommunist who supported HUAC's mission. Robinson remembers the Deacon assuring him that his participation "would be the final stroke necessary to establish forever the Negro's place in baseball—and possibly in America."

Interestingly, the dilemma arrived in just the year that Robinson was seeking to transition from his popular persona of an unassuming, nonthreatening figure (under his original pledge to Rickey in the first two years with the Dodgers) to his more natural tone of a fiery, impassioned, outspoken one. The reason that HUAC imagined him as the marquee witness for the hearings no doubt capitalized in part on white America's impression of Robinson in his 1947 to 1948 incarnation as complaisant (to bathe themselves in the national good feelings for the baseball star through publicity, committee members dispensed with the normal rules that restricted photographs).

As he contemplated whether to take his more aggressive stance into the heady world of Washington politics, he had to weigh personally not only his own potentially damaging past personal associations but also the endangering of the public favor that had allowed his rise in baseball. There was the additional recognition that the person to which he might contribute harm was not an inconsequential figure to African Americans: "Rae and I remembered how, as children, we had thrilled to Robeson's success, had hummed the tunes made famous by his booming bass-baritone voice." While he characterized Robeson as "bitter" (an implicit contrast to the public's impression of a more contented, acquiescent Robinson), he well understood how the older entertainer had arrived at that psychological condition. "Now a white man from Georgia was asking *me*, a 'refugee' from Georgia," he recalled, "to denounce Robeson, who spoke from a well of bitterness that few white people ever would understand. Thus white Americans would not understand my dilemma, or that of any Negro faced with the task of passing judgment on Robeson."

In the end, Robinson did go to Washington. He was an opponent of communism, largely due to its disaffection for his religious faith. He was further "afraid that Robeson's statement might discredit blacks in the eyes of whites. . . . I felt that there were two wars raging at once—one against foreign enemies and one against domestic foes—and the black man was forced to fight against both. I felt we must not back down on either front." He also came to resent the unrelenting pressure to refuse HUAC that came from quarters as important as the NAACP (which reminded him that it had long "been critical of this committee's methods, activities, [and] procedures"). Later he indicated that "it was that attempt to keep me quiet that made me decide to go ahead and do it." He delivered a statement that had been shaped by Rickey and Lester Granger (head of the National Urban League and a prior cooperative HUAC witness). While he denounced Robeson's statement as unrepresentative of himself and the clear majority of African Americans, he defended the baritone's "right to his personal views." Robinson did make sure to emphasize that the "fact that it is a Communist who denounces injustice in the courts, police brutality and lynching when it happens doesn't change the truth of his charges. . . . Negroes were stirred up long before there was a Communist Party, and they'll stay stirred up long after the Party has disappeared—unless Jim Crow has disappeared by then as well."

The following morning brought broad praise from the white press. The *New York Times* carried a front-page article with his entire remarks printed inside, and the *New York Post* carried a statement excerpt on its editorial page under the title, "Credo of an American." HUAC members themselves had lauded his "splendid statement." More mixed were African American media, some praising him for landing a blow against racism with his statement, and others noting unease among some black leaders over his participation. As for Robeson, he saved his criticism for HUAC, hewing closely to Robinson's original concern that he not "fall prey to the white man's game and allow myself to be pitted against another black man." "I have no quarrel with Jackie," he told the press. "I have a great deal of respect for him. He is entitled to his views. I feel that the House Committee has insulted Jackie, it has insulted me, it has insulted the entire Negro race." Of course, one of the many risky moves that Robeson had taken in his career was to advocate openly at the 1943 baseball owners' meeting for just the integration that Jackie Robinson had enjoyed. In fact, Robeson celebrated Robinson's signing by Rickey two years later as "the greatest step ever taken by organized baseball on behalf of the American Negro."

Robeson, already being squeezed by negative publicity through concert cancellations and picketing, suffered another blow a month later in the upstate town of Peekskill, New York. Scheduled to deliver a benefit performance for the left-leaning Civil Rights Congress, local veterans were roused to action by the recent national headlines and reactionary editorials in the local *Evening Star*, which claimed he had recently "turned loudly and violently pro-Russian." Some three hundred local veterans descended on the concertgoers, wreaking havoc on both them and the concert grounds and equipment. As the attendees fled in terror, veterans concealed themselves along the escape route, where they had placed roadblocks of logs, rocks, and barbed wire. Slowed considerably, the would-be audience members became subject to further attacks, including hurled stones.

The next morning Bill Mardo, of the Communist newspaper *The Daily Worker*, delivered the news about Peekskill to Robinson in the Dodger clubhouse. Shaken, with "anger written all over his face," according to Mardo, he lamented, "Paul Robeson should have the right to sing, speak, or do anything he wants to. Those mobs make it tough on everyone. It's Robeson's right to do or be or say as he believes." Then, turning the rhetorical tables on the eager pursuers of American leftists, he remarked, "I think those rioters ought to be investigated, and let's find out if what they did is supposed to be the democratic way of doing things." Still a confirmed anticommunist, he admonished, "Anything progressive is called communism."

But for Robeson, that was hardly the end. His once bright career was severely damaged. Music promoters canceled eighty-five of his concerts in 1949 and 1950 alone. In the years thereafter, even scheduling concerts for the once highly sought-after artist would prove difficult, as his earnings dropped from $104,000 per year to a paltry $6,000. Biographies on the great singer were banned from libraries, and his recordings were withdrawn from record stores. When the State Department revoked his passport in 1950, even the possibility of finding more receptive progressive audiences abroad evaporated. Professionally inactive for eight years until his passport was renewed, he then found his performance options significantly limited, and he suffered from bouts of depression before retiring from public life in 1963. Robeson's now reclusive life ended thirteen years later.

Time would further sober Robinson's view of his participation in the Robeson hearing. At a Dodgers players' party a few years later, the player was heard to regret the pressure that swayed him to testify. "If Mr. Rickey at that time had asked me to jump headfirst off the Brooklyn Bridge," he remarked, "I would have done it." In his autobiography published in the last year of his life, Robinson recalled having at the time of his HUAC testimony "much more faith in the ultimate justice of the American white man than I have today. I would reject such an invitation if offered now." "I have grown wiser and closer to painful truths about America's destructiveness," he continued, "[a]nd I do have an increased respect for Paul Robeson who over the span of that twenty years [since Robinson made his HUAC appearance], sacrificed himself, his career, and the wealth and comfort he once enjoyed because, I believe, he was sincerely trying to help his people."

Happy to be back to playing baseball, Jackie Robinson and the Dodgers headed to Vero Beach, Florida in the spring of 1950 with broad expectations to win the National League. Jackie also brought with him a newly signed contract, making him the highest paid player in Dodger history at $35,000. Brooklyn took the National League lead in May, but he began to falter by July, concluding the season with a deciding, season-ending series against the Philadelphia Phillies. The Phillies would capture the final game in extra innings and, thus, the pennant in an exciting but disappointing end to the Dodgers' hopes. Despite the team's fortunes, Robinson had another impressive year, batting .328, winning a spot on the midseason All-Star team, and further cementing his recognized role as team leader. "He's the indispensable man," said Dodger coach Jake Pitler.

Branch Rickey, who had been clearly indispensable to Robinson, however, was on his way out of the Brooklyn front office. The death of John L. Smith, who controlled one-quarter of the club, shook up ownership arrangements. Fellow co-owner Walter O'Malley (the team's vice president and chief counsel who had long-simmering disputes with Rickey) acquired Smith's shares, leaving one-half of the Dodgers now in O'Malley's possession. Rickey, still clinging to his one-quarter ownership share and in debt troubles, felt forced to sell his portion to O'Malley. That left the taciturn O'Malley in control and in no mood to renew the Mahatma's expiring general manager contract that October. So determined was O'Malley to rid the team of Rickey's influence that mentioning Rickey's name in the Dodger office brought a $1 fine.

The Deacon, long respected as an innovative baseball administrator, landed on his feet, as general manager of the Pittsburgh Pirates. After several seasons finishing in the cellar of the standings, Rickey left Pittsburgh in 1959. He then served briefly as a consultant for the Cardinals before retiring for good in 1964, just a year before his death.

Remaining behind in Brooklyn was the considerably displeased Jackie Robinson. The news "hit me hard," he conceded, and brought to an end to the professional relationship they had enjoyed. Continuing would be a very warm, essentially paternal relationship Robinson enjoyed with his former manager. The second baseman wrote Rickey that it had "been the finest experience I have had being associated with you, and I want to thank you very much for all you have meant not only to me and my family but to the entire country and particularly the members of our race." Expressing a desire to conclude his career in Brooklyn, Robinson noted that "if I have to go any place I hope it can be with you." He concluded with the hope that he and his wife "can always be regarded as your friends and whenever we need advice we can call you as usual regardless of where we may be." That desire would certainly be fulfilled, as the two men retained a close friendship throughout their lives. Rickey's grandson, Branch B. Rickey, recalls that "sometimes my family believed that my grandfather really had two sons—my father and Jackie. We all accepted it as a fact of our lives; we knew that my grandfather loved Jackie, and we all respected Jackie."

Robinson, having lost his paternal partner in the integration enterprise, found his new general manager Walter O'Malley "viciously antagonistic" to him. Knowing that he "felt very deeply about Mr. Rickey," charged Robinson, "I became the target of [O'Malley's] insecurity." Robinson's newfound outspokenness did not endear him to the employer. Under O'Malley, the Dodgers would do their early conditioning at the usual Vero Beach complex but would move to Miami to play their exhibition games. This meant returning to segregated accommodations, most unwelcome to the now highly accomplished Robinson, who had hoped enough dues had been paid to put such humiliations safely behind him. An accompanying Rachel recalls "sitting on a rickety old 'colored' bus with Jackie Junior and seeing some of the white Dodger women staring at us as we drove off to our colored and quite unequal hotel." The issue would flare into an argument when O'Malley summoned Jackie and Rachel to his office to chastise them for "reports that you've been complaining about having to stay in a separate hotel in Miami. That was good enough for you in 1947. Why do you have to make trouble now?" Jackie instructed his white manager that "I took a lot of things in 1947, not because I felt that they were good enough for me, but because I was convinced that it was important enough to me and to some of the things I wanted to see come about in baseball for me to grin and bear some things that I never was really able to stomach. I happen to feel now, though, that there are a lot of insults being suffered by Negro ballplayers that wouldn't be necessary if the owners would show a little bit more courage."

He reminded O'Malley that he had actually held his tongue about the inferior quality and segregation of their hotel, and had only complained about their children's room not adjoining to theirs—which brought worries about their welfare across the hall. "[I]t doesn't strike me too well," he admonished his superior, "to have people who sit in comfort in an air-conditioned hotel lecture to me about not complaining about where I live." A chastened O'Malley turned diplomatic, as he "seemed surprised by the response he had received, at the fact that neither Rae nor I was frightened or awed. . . . Rae and I left that meeting in a most unhappy mood . . . O'Malley wanted 'yes men' around him, and he would appreciate a Negro only if he were the smiling, congenial, hat-in-hand kind."

Despite Robinson's personal unease about the front office, the Dodgers seemed to take the 1951 season by storm, commanding a thirteen-game lead in mid-August. Then came the infamous late charge by the hated New York Giants, who won thirty-seven of their last forty-four games and tied with Brooklyn on the season's final day. This set up a day of Dodger baseball infamy when they played the Giants in a now renowned three-game series for the league pennant. The teams split the first two games, bringing the deciding game to the Giants' Polo Grounds stadium. Brooklyn carried a 3–1 lead into the final inning before the Giants' Bobby Thomson drove one of the most legendary home runs in the history of baseball over the fence—dubbed "the shot heard 'round the world"—sealing one of the most bitter disappointments in Dodgers' history.

Robinson had another strong year in 1952, helping to guide his team to the league championship. Yet again Brooklyn faced the Yankees in the World Series—the third occasion in Robinson's six years in the Majors. While taking the Yanks to seven games, the Dodgers were on the losing end again. Jackie played without distinction, gaining only four hits in twenty-three at-

Figure 6.1.   Robinson at the plate. *Source*: Library of Congress, http://www.loc.gov/ item/97518921/

bats, and failing to take base in the bases-loaded seventh inning of the final game. Still, Jackie was pleased to see another African American Dodger win the season's Rookie of the Year Award, pitcher Joe Black.

Robinson's offseason activities had continued to expand, and now he opened the Jackie Robinson Store, catering in men's clothing, in December. Situated in Harlem's well-known shopping district near the Hotel Theresa and Apollo Theater, he spent considerable time there to draw customers. He also purchased eight acres in the Bronx, intending to construct low-income apartment buildings. Neither venture did well, with Robinson selling his share of the store six years later. He had already branched out to do some offseason TV and radio broadcasts. In 1950, he even starred in *The Jackie Robinson Story*, a Hollywood film production of his life in baseball. By now, he had grown especially conscious of the fact that his sporting years would be limited. "I'm no longer a young man," he reminded the press. "I'm trying to save money for when my legs give out."

Just before the dawn of the 1953 season, *Sport* magazine published an article focused on the rising concern over Robinson's aggressive stance. The title, "Why They Boo Jackie Robinson," came from a poignant query the player himself offered up to a reporter late in the previous season: "What do you think of the booing? Why are they booing me?" Written sympathetically by local *New York Post* reporter Milton Gross, the story called Jackie "combative," "emotional," and "calculating," and conceded that "he is being accused of being a pop-off, a whiner, a sulker, a showboat and a troublemaker." Opposing fans, said the journalist, "have begun to boo Robinson systematically and unmercifully." "If he is touchy," asked Gross, "who can blame him? Who else was asked to enter the major leagues wearing an emotional straitjacket. . . . If he is sensitive, maybe it is because what he has gained has not come easily, but only through suffering and sufferance. Maybe it is because he has been victimized too often, in his own mind, by bad raps."

The article sought to address the public's growing unease with the more open and aggressive post-1948 Robinson. Jackie had begun to speak candidly to both white opponents and umpires in a way unthinkable in his first two years in the Majors. "He was the most difficult ballplayer I had to deal with," one of the latter claimed in his memoir. When his relationship with the officials seemed to sour, he attributed much of the problem to racism, feeling that they were rankling at behavior they would deem acceptable in white players. The infielder claimed that "as long as I appeared to ignore insult and injury, I was a martyred hero to a lot of people," but "the minute I began to sound-off—I became a swell-head, wise guy, an 'uppity' nigger." Behavior thought "inappropriate to a black man" would merely be seen as "spirited" when exhibited by a white player, he asserted.

The difficult chemistry of succeeding as a black ballplayer had always been playing aggressively enough on the diamond to advance the scoreboard without offending white sensibilities. "He played like hell," recalled journalist Roger Kahn, "hitting, running, stealing home, sticking his jaw into an umpire's face with no apology for being black, none at all." In the summer of 1950, he publicly called on National League president Ford Frick to intervene. "Frick has given [umpires] too much power," he insisted. "Something's going to have to be done about it." Dodgers coach Clyde Sukeforth hastened to the player's defense: "There is no question in my mind that the umpires are picking on Robinson." Admitting that Robinson could challenge officials' calls at times, he claimed, "[I]f Robinson were somebody else, no umpire would pay any attention." One journalist recalled one official ejecting Robinson for merely wincing at second base at a closely called pitch.

Robinson's more combative behavior only reinforced the already present frustrations with containing the player on the field. His pesky tactics on the base paths had long drove opposing pitchers literally to the kind of dangerous distraction that produced bad pitches. Journalist Roger Kahn recalled that Robinson not only "beat you . . . he'd frustrate you. He made teams angry." But there was an increasing edge to Robinson's play as well, which may have crossed the line of mere overcompetitiveness to a modest silent repayment to his racist detractors: "[O]nce in a while, he would steal home when the Dodgers were five runs ahead, and he would stick it to you. And, of course, personally he would needle very hard."

His relationship with the press also became strained. Cleveland's local sports page charged Robinson with becoming a "rabble rouser" on a "soap box." The *Sporting News* regularly called for Robinson's censure under such headlines as "A Problem Grows in Brooklyn" and "Robinson Should Be a Player, Not a Crusader." The journalistic reprimands even spread to black newspapers, as the *Pittsburgh Courier* charged he had become "obsessed with his own importance," and another claiming that the player "isn't as popular in the press box as he once was." In fact, when the United Press International announced their 1950 all-star team, the sportswriters had suspiciously selected the Giants' Eddie Stanky over Robinson at second base. The former player's numbers were inferior in every major category, and Stanky was—like the man he beat—known for his aggressive play, but his white skin made his combativeness apparently more acceptable to the public.

Adding to the discontent, many reporters still insisted Robinson be held to a higher standard of public approval long after baseball segregation had been broken. The *Sporting News* expected him to "be beyond reproach," and it continued to rebuke his outspokenness as a sign of ungrateful disregard that he owed "a great deal to the game." Black teammate Roy Campanella expanded the criticism by stating, "Instead of being grateful to baseball, he's criticizing it. Everything he has he owes to baseball." For his part, Jackie rightly noted that baseball had made far more financially from his presence than he retained in his paychecks. "The way I figured it," he claimed, "I was even with baseball and baseball was even with me."

Defenders asserted that the surprisingly aggressive Robinson emerged from the sublimated frustration of remaining unnaturally quiet in his first two seasons. "I had too much stored up inside me," he maintained. Hall of Fame pitcher Don Drysdale, who arrived on the team late in Jackie's career, saw "an awfully intense man. I could see the frustrations he had to endure, and the battle scars." Robinson clearly was aggressive on the field "because that was his style," but he had to simultaneously "sit there and take a lot of crap. Try that sometime," he challenged. Others saw this more tempestuous Robinson not as the distorted outcome of a two-year pressure cooker, but simply the real man finally emerging. Noting the outspokenness and combativeness could be seen in the player's younger years, journalist Roger Kahn asserted that it "was this fury of Robinson's that enabled him to do the great and immensely difficult thing that he did" (i.e., being the first black player in the Majors). His wife, Rachel, commonly depicted as the picture of quiet grace, remembers being raised to be "as ladylike as possible. I was taught not to be aggressive. And then, marrying Jack I was in the middle of a struggle where—well, without aggressive behavior it would have failed. There was an aggressiveness to Jack's whole career in baseball. It was a kind of objection to the white society."

Still, despite the public discomfort with Robinson's later years in the game, one can only wonder at the unseen burdens he carried alone. Rachel Robinson claimed the only way she could detect when the pressure was mounting on her husband was that he would head for the back lawn with a bucket of golf balls and begin "driving them into the lake" one by one. When a reporter questioned the player on the story, "Jack gave me a twinkly look. 'The golf balls are white,' he said."

If Robinson might have modified his approach to win over his detractors, some of what he had to say surely would have rankled even if sugarcoated. He ran particularly afoul of white sensitivities in 1953 when asked to address

New Yorkers' beloved Yankees' racial recalcitrance. Appearing on a local television talk show, an audience member asked if he thought the team's front office was discriminatory against black players. Clarifying that the Yankee players were "wonderful gentlemen" that he did not accuse of racism, his simple affirmative reply highlighted that management continued to drag their feet and fielded the city's only all-white team. Incensed Yankee general manger George Weiss mystifyingly maintained his club would include an African American once one could be identified who could "play good enough ball to win a place." The team, however, would not countenance the inclusion of a black player "just for exploitation." Robinson's remarks stirred a series of columns critical of the player, "many hate letters," and a phone call from baseball commissioner Ford Frick demanding an explanation. Jack stood by his statement, though.

Highlighting this growing unhappiness with the "new" Robinson was whites' affection for his much more conciliatory black teammate, Roy Campanella. Whites' warmth for the affable catcher gave them an opportunity to declaim any racism for their discomfort with Robinson's newfound assertiveness. In a clear contrast to Robinson, Campanella publicly assured whites that he was no "crusader."

When Branch Rickey informed Campanella, for example, that he would begin the 1948 season with the Minor League St. Paul club, he attempted to console the player with the reminder that he would "pioneer the Negroes into the American Association." A dutiful Campanella consented to go agreeably "because it's in my contract" to follow management directives, but he informed the Deacon that he was "a ballplayer, not a pioneer," who noted only the color of a player's uniform.

The white Dodger players found Campanella's less intense off-field manner a welcome respite from Robinson's more determined demeanor. Harold Parrott, the team's traveling secretary, recalled bringing food to the two black players, sequestered outside by segregation while their white teammates enjoyed their road trip meal inside. Campanella urged a livid Robinson to contain himself: "Let's not have no trouble, Jackie. This is the onliest thing we can do right now, 'lessen we want to go back to them crummy Negro leagues." In the ensuing years when young black Dodgers chafed at discriminatory treatment, he reminded, "You're in the big league now. It's nice up here. You're getting an opportunity to show what you can do—don't louse it up for everyone else." Asked by reporters about the rising tide of the civil rights movement later, he said only, "I'm a colored man. I know there are things I can do and things I can't do without stirring up some people. But a few years ago there were many more things I couldn't do than I can do today. I'm willing to wait. All this came by waiting." The scars of civil rights activists might say differently. So might the psychological burdens borne by his pathbreaking teammate. And, surely Campanella's ability to reap the benefits of Robinson's impatience to clear the base paths for black players to follow—while claiming such insistence merely irritated good relations—must have rankled Robinson.

The white press's clear preference for Campanella's more compliant persona only added to the strain. The Dodger catcher "seems to have realized that inborn prejudices cannot be eradicated overnight," the New York Times's Roscoe McGowen wrote approvingly. "When I talk to Campy I almost never think of him as a Negro," admired the Daily News's Dick Young. Apparently oblivious to the racial predilections that the white writer himself brought to the conversation, Young scolded Robinson: "Any time I talk to you, I'm acutely aware of the fact that you're a Negro." "I can go to Campy and all we discuss is baseball. I talk to you and sooner or later we get around to social issues," Young chastised. But Jackie was quick to note his black teammate was clearly viewed an African American "when he was Jim Crowed at the Adams Hotel in St. Louis" during southern spring training, and "when he goes to buy a house." What Young clearly implied, countered Robinson, was "that he didn't think of [Campanella] as a certain kind of Negro." Jackie had no interest in being the "whining, cringing, handkerchief-head standing before you with his hat in his hand," he told the press. He was perfectly satisfied in being regarded "as the kind of Negro who's come to the conclusion that he isn't going to beg for anything, that he will be reasonable but he damned well is tired of being patient," and would simply live with making "some people uncomfortable." At the end of his life, he confided to a journalist his view that Campanella had "a little [Uncle] Tom in him."

African American sportswriter Doc Young lamented the need to compare the two black all-stars, claiming they simply had different personalities. Campanella, he contended, "believes in 'getting along' at all costs, in being exceedingly grateful" for his Major League shot. Robinson, claimed the black journalist, "is an aggressive individualist who is willing to pay the price" for his difficult achievements in a white world. Campanella further claimed that his field position required him to be "a jolly fellow." Since a catcher must periodically correct the pitcher's approach during the game, Campanella needed "a piece of sugar in [his] hand" and a "sunny disposition" when delivering the vital criticism in the midst of the contest. No doubt an African American might need *extra* sugar when correcting a white man in 1940s America.

While Robinson still held Rickey in high regard, he was clear-eyed that most Major League clubs' commitment to black players related to on-field statistics and ticket sales primarily and not to societal progress. "Jackie knows that baseball never has been overly concerned about its unpaid debts to all the great Negro players" who never had a shot at the big leagues, claimed Young. In short, Campanella comfortingly reminded whites of accommodating blacks of the old racial caste system. Robinson's insubmission embodied the unsettling future of racial change to come. If whites had hoped they could control racial change by measuredly cracking open the door of opportunity to blacks, Jackie Robinson's resolute calls for more would be simply the first unsettling signal in the decades to come.

The 1953 season would prove to be one of the most productive for Robinson and his team. His numbers driving in runs came second only to his 1949 campaign, and the Dodgers made it to the World Series for a second consecutive year—unfortunately losing once again to their crosstown rivals, the Yankees. The following season, however, proved to be a disappointment, as the Dodgers finished second in the National League and Robinson failed to live up to the now lofty expectations created by his previous play. His growing tension with the press and public also escalated that year. A June incident marked the low point. Angered over an ejection, Jackie tossed his bat—slickened by falling rain—in the direction of the dugout, only to have it slip further all the way into the stands. Although no spectators were apparently injured and the observing umpire called it an accident, the episode received nationwide negative coverage, and ensured that fans jeered him throughout the summer. *Sport* magazine called the Dodger great that year "the most savagely booed, intensively criticized, ruthlessly libeled player in the game."

Rumors—which had begun as early as 1953—continued to circulate that Dodgers president Walter O'Malley was considering trading Robinson. The *Pittsburgh Courier* claimed that the club executive was "fed up with Jackie's insistence on getting into fights on and off the field." The player later wrote that he too "was getting fed up" at the close of the 1954 season "and I began to make preparations to leave baseball. I loved the game but my experience had not been typical—I was tired of fighting the press, the front office—and I knew that I was reaching the end of my peak years as an athlete." He contemplated an "administrative job" in baseball, but he concluded that chance "was mighty slim." In a possible reference to the Campanella comparisons, he surmised his opportunities would have been better had he "been easy-going, willing to be meek and humble."

Robinson's final two seasons, 1955 and 1956, only further demonstrated the player's gradual decline, as his game appearances receded and the former all-star was shuttled to different infield positions. This added up to mounting frustration for Robinson, who lashed out in the press at his manager when benched before the start of the 1955 season. "When I'm fit I've got as much right to be playing as any man on this team. [Dodgers manager Walter Alston] knows it—or maybe he doesn't," he growled. The escalating tension almost brought the two men to blows in the exhibition season, before Campanella interceded. Despite the off-field turmoil, Robinson did work his way into the 1955 lineup for 105 games, and performed admirably to help his team to its first ever World Series championship against the dreaded Yankees. He could also look with pride on his impact: forty African Americans now played in the Major Leagues, with only three clubs maintaining an all-white roster.

Robinson, despite nagging injuries, contributed significantly to a 1956 late stretch run by Brooklyn to win the National League on the final day of that season. A New York sportswriter called Jackie "still the most dangerous individual competitor in the game." Facing the Yankees yet again, the Dodgers managed to force the World Series into seven games before they lost.

Having already contemplated retirement a year prior, Robinson weighed it more seriously after the 1956 season. To ready himself for the idea, he increased his community work, and entertained conversations with the business world. With regard to the former, Jackie accepted the NAACP's Spingarn Medal in December 1956—the first athlete recipient. The group's highest award, it honors an African American who has brought credit to the race. He took the occasion of the banquet to further defend his embattled reputation in his later playing years. Many had cautioned him "not to speak up every time I thought there was an injustice," he told the audience. The "biting criticism" had sometimes taken its toll, and "many times I have been told that I should just let things work themselves out without involving myself in them. If I did so, many honors and awards would come my way." His determination to persevere despite the lure of such easy public praise, he claimed, had led him to the more satisfying NAACP's award ceremony that night.

Jackie's increasing lean toward retirement was hastened by a career opportunity with the coffee shop chain, Chock Full o'Nuts. CEO William Black

Figure 6.2. Robinson speaks with NAACP Executive Secretary Roy Wilkins (center) and jazz legend Duke Ellington, after receiving the organization's highest honor, the Springarn Medal Award, 1956. Paul Robeson had won the honor in 1945, and Dr. Martin Luther King Jr. was the 1957 receipient.

was looking for a new personnel director, and he quickly offered the position to the Dodger legend in early December 1956. This meant renewing conversations with *Look* magazine. The periodical had reached agreement with Robinson two years prior that he would announce his retirement through their publication. His $50,000 fee included a lengthy interview. To ensure maximum publicity and interest for the piece, *Look* editors insisted that his public retirement announcement occur simultaneously when the magazine hit newsstands.

Aware that his advanced age of thirty-eight meant his playing days were numbered, Robinson eagerly moved on to the coffee giant's offer amid renewed trade rumors. "There's no sentiment in baseball," he later wrote. "You start slipping, and pretty soon they're moving you around like a used car." Moments after affixing his signature to an employment contract, he returned a call to the Dodgers front office. This time the speculation was true: he had been traded to the New York Giants. This now put him in an awkward position when contacted by the Giants. He told the team that he would "be glad to play" for them, should he not retire—a decision he would announce in a few weeks. While his comments were all above board, the Giants management did not foresee receiving their answer on the cover of *Look* magazine. An irate Dodgers management—with whom Robinson had had prickly relations since the firing of his mentor Rickey—spewed anger in the sports pages, calling him ungrateful, angling for a higher salary, and "always seeking publicity." Although the player angrily defended himself from the "unwarranted criticism," his wife, Rachel, admitted decades later to the couple's hidden pleasure at the brouhaha: "There was a kind of revenge in it for us," she conceded. "We felt that the top people had hurt us, and we were getting back a little at them."

Many players and journalists, though, gave the Dodger legend his due recognition. Popular New York sportswriter Jimmy Cannon gave an especially insightful reminiscence: "You are Jackie Robinson who is consumed by rage and pride. You're a complicated man, persecuted by slanderous myths, using anger as a confederate. No athlete of any time has been assaulted by such an aching loneliness which created your personality and shaped your genuine greatness." And with that, Jack Roosevelt Robinson left the field.

By then, all but three Major League clubs had integrated their rosters. (One more did so in each of the following consecutive years, making the recalcitrant Boston Red Sox the last domino to fall to racial justice in 1959.) The process was never as smooth as many whites would like to recall. Black players on the Minor League and Major League level would continue to endure fan racism, discriminatory treatment on team trips, and physical danger on the diamond. Between 1949 and 1951, for example, at least six African American players were carried off the field by stretcher due to white hurlers' pitches.

Negro League clubs were also casualties of the integration process. Only two years after Robinson took the field in Brooklyn, Negro League attendance had dropped so significantly that the New York Black Yankees and the more storied Newark Eagles disbanded. Eagles owner Effa Manley had warned earlier that season, "The livelihoods, the careers, the families of 400 Negro ballplayers are in jeopardy because four players were successful in getting into the Major Leagues." The Homestead Grays—one of the most renowned of the black teams—withdrew its formal ties to the Negro Leagues and became simply a barnstorming unit in the same year. This caused the Negro National League to collapse, with the remaining three teams to join a reconstituted ten-team Negro American League. By 1951, the toll of integration and—especially the loss of premier black players to white clubs—left the Negro League with only six teams. Two years later, two more had disappeared.

By then, black baseball had tried a number of different approaches to keep itself aloft. Ironically, just as Major League teams began to integrate, some Negro League teams moved to the segregated South, where the white Majors had no presence to find a more captive black audience. In 1946, the Cleveland Buckeyes took the unorthodox approach of signing a white player. Pitcher Eddie Klep, who had performed well in semipro ball, became the first white man to play in the Negro Leagues. While holding to white supremacy, Birmingham proved at least equal in its enforcement when it refused to allow Klep to play in an exhibition game that would have integrated the field in reverse. In the end, however, it was not racism that doomed Klep's stint with black baseball but his middling talent. He was released in June. In 1953, the Indianapolis Clowns signed the Negro Leagues' first female player, causing black journalist Wendell Smith to remark that "Negro baseball has collapsed to the extent it must tie itself to a woman's apron strings in order to survive." Other teams followed suit when attendance spiked, but public interest in the experiment proved fleeting. By 1953, the Negro American League had become essentially a barnstorming operation, with only a handful of games actually rendered on the teams' home fields.

In 1955, the Indianapolis Clowns, the largest draw in black baseball, formally withdrew from the Negro League and became simply an independent team. This was a crippling blow to the flagging fortunes of organized black baseball, but it appeared to be a sound business move for the Clowns. Rather than saddling itself with a league schedule, the club was now free to simply seek the largest paydays. It could now also fully pursue its long-used comedic angle, which—as the talent waned in black ball—had become its biggest selling point. The return of between-innings bits playing to comic stereotypes such as the "Saturday Night Whore" was a sad spectacle to many African American critics as the team desperately hung on. It patterned itself after the more successful, and family friendly, traveling black basketballers, the Harlem Globetrotters. The Clowns mined this approach until their surprisingly late demise in the early 1980s.

The Negro Leagues saw their wimpering end in 1963, long past the point many once-loyal African American fans knew they still existed. Some observers had pled with the black public to preserve the institution in the early years of the sport's integration. Just as Jackie Robinson's rise to white baseball was a significant factor to prepare the country for the prospect of full desegregation, black baseball's failing health was the canary in the coalmine. Those African American enterprises that had thrived in the old world of segregation would suffer stifling competition from the white businesses that began to welcome African American customers.

The *Pittsburgh Courier*'s William Webster recognized blacks' growing distaste for separate institutions, but cautioned that "Negro baseball is a Negro business and . . . it needs preserving equally as much as Negro insurance companies, groceries, and bars." Webster, and others who could take the temperature of black America, knew they must battle against the new black enthusiasm for taking their affections and dollars to white businesses. For many African Americans, Robinson's very ascension to the white ranks meant the increasing chance of finally more freely participating in American life and commerce. Thus, Webster sought to remind readers of the future cost of these changes: "[A]nother of our enterprises is about to fold. Is this progress?" he asked. Philadelphia radio host and activist Georgie Woods looked back on the period with some regret: "We had black hotels, we had our own restaurants, our own shopping centers, our own clothing stores— and we lost it all through integration." Black Power spokesmen would pick up this cudgel again, but that was several years away from view.

Other analysts have provided rejoinders of these losses as rose-colored nostalgia. Some of these businesses in the black community were actually owned by whites. The Negro Leagues' acclaimed Kansas City Monarchs are an instructive example. Some knowingly took advantage of the commercial "shelter" provided them by segregation. Since African Americans might have nowhere else to go, some unscrupulous black businessmen offered inferior products at inflated prices. A 1950 *Pittsburgh Courier* editorial criticized black businesses (including baseball) for trying to ride simply on the race loyalty of its African American clientele without seeking to competitively improve. "Jackie Robinson was helped over the hurdle from Negro baseball to major league baseball. What about major league business?" the black newspaper inquired. "Are Negro businessmen only competent to cater to a trade based on race prejudice?"

And yet, while it seems difficult to deny that African Americans' employment prospects considerably brightened in the long run by this national project of desegregation, there were disheartening casualties along the way. The next major venue of desegregation came in public schools—a rocky, lengthy road at best, which took at least a decade and a half to finalize (followed by largely resegregating through white flight and many wealthier whites' shift to private schools in the decades to come). And as those unified school districts finally streamlined the unnecessarily bloated dual systems into one, it was commonplace to eliminate black administrators and teachers. Hence, even the heralded *Brown v. Board of Education* decision created unintended detritus in the lives of highly educated and once proud black educational professionals.

Baseball, of course, created a detritus all its own. Like Jackie Robinson's brother, Mack, the vast majority of the once towering sportsmen of the defunct Negro Leagues found themselves caught between the limbo of segregation and a dawning age white baseball managers considered them too old to begin. Cool Papa Bell, considered by many experts to be one of the fastest to ever play the game, eeked out a living as a custodian and security guard. Jimmie Crutchfield, a perpetual All-Star outfielder, took a position with the post office. Buck Leonard, who batted behind Josh Gibson on the legendary Homestead Grays to form one of the best teams to ever take a diamond, became a real estate salesman. Hilton Smith, owner of an impossible curve ball but overshadowed by the more flamboyant Satchel Paige, picked up a teaching job.

There was also the emotional loss that cannot be calculated in a box score. Former pitcher for the Negro Leagues' Philadelphia Stars Tom Johnson never made it to the Majors, but could still take pride that "in the absence of the opportunity [to participate in Major League baseball], the blacks created that opportunity, created . . . a baseball world for themselves, so they could demonstrate their abilities." Furthermore, the Major Leagues would never replace the resonance and impact of the Negro League teams' prominent presence for the black communities they called home. African American poet and activist Amiri Baraka, who grew up on the Newark Eagles, called black baseball "like a light somewhere . . . connected to laughter and self-love."

CHAPTER SEVEN

~

Robinson Off the Diamond

His pathbreaking career on the diamond now over, Jackie Robinson found himself once again a black man in a white man's world. Having made his mark in the arena most open to African Americans—sports and entertainment—he now was forced to find his way in the "real world" of 1950s America. Robinson was not entirely unprepared for the transition, however.

For years, he had taken on a variety of business opportunities beyond the baseball park. As early as his second year in the Majors, Robinson hosted a daily radio show in New York City during the offseason. He addressed both sports and—in a break with tradition for a black man—social issues. His favorite guest would be his old idol, boxer Joe Louis, whom he praised for making it "easy for me and the other fellows now in baseball. . . . I have tried to follow his footsteps." Robinson would expand his media presence to a television program in the following year. In 1950, the feature film *The Jackie Robinson Story* was released. He wrangled with studios that insisted the film could only be made if it followed the formula: the star should be a white man teaching Robinson how to be a great player. Standing his ground, the studio finally agreed to shoot the script with Robinson himself as the lead. The resulting low-budget film was hardly a masterpiece, but its patriotic themes (including the repeated background score of "America the Beautiful," and the conclusion with Robinson's HUAC testimony with the Statue of Liberty silhouetted behind) mostly advanced his popular image. His "Jackie Robinson Houses" development united his interest in the business world and aiding fellow African American families. A New York City real estate developer contributed the start-up funding in 1952, as Robinson sought to build a profitable enterprise that would also provide needed homes for working-class black families in poor areas of the metropolitan area. Later that year, he opened the Jackie Robinson Store in Harlem's busy shopping district. The men's clothing shop, however, was never profitable.

Having dabbled in a variety of commercial opportunities, Robinson was now more immediately concerned with a steadier source of income as he contemplated retirement. Before he pulled the trigger on his decision to step down, the Dodgers star had already secured the next chapter of his life: as a personnel executive with the coffee and restaurant chain, Chock Full o'Nuts. CEO William Black, who felt Robinson was "just the man for the job," had engaged in quiet negotiations before the star's baseball retirement was declared. Robinson readily agreed, both because of the generous salary and the opportunity to shepherd a largely black workforce.

The ethnic composition of Chock's employees had actually been a point of criticism, with some whites accusing Black of employment discrimination against whites, referring to the corporation as "Chock Full o'Niggers." The

Figure 7.1. Jackie Robinson with Chock Full o'Nuts founder William Black. *Source:* **Chock Full o'Nuts Marketing Dept photo.**

complaints became loud enough that Black felt forced to take out full-page newspaper ads defending his company's equal hiring practices. (Less laudatory may have been Black's explanation in the ads that he had arrived at the firm's 80 percent black majority partly because they were willing to take the lower wages being offered.) Later, as Robinson's growing outspokenness on racial matters created some rattled white nerves, Black admirably told the press, "If anyone wants to boycott 'Chock' because I hired Jackie Robinson, I recommend Martinson's coffee. It's just as good. As for our restaurants, there are Nedick's, Bickford's and Horn and Hardart in our price range. Try them. You may even like them better than ours."

Robinson found purpose in aiding and enabling Chock's primarily African American employees, and saw to it that a new flyer was given to all workers shortly after he began. "As to job security: No employee will be dismissed," it promised, "without the right to present his or her case to Mr. Jackie Robinson, our Vice-President in Charge of Personnel." He soon visited most of the company restaurants to meet and converse personally with the line staff. "This is a team operation," he claimed, using language he carried from the baseball field. "To gain the confidence of employees, you must be willing to discuss their problems openly with them."

Still, Black was a businessman, and Robinson's notoriety obviously brought certain advantages. The sports star was, recalled one company vice president, a "tremendous feather in [Black's] cap. Jackie was such a celebrity." Such natural popularity might help mitigate a growing concern among Chock leaders: labor union talk. Black apparently hoped that his mostly African American workforce would feel newfound loyalty to the front office, which now included a celebrated champion of their race. "I hired Jackie because a majority of the people who work for me are colored," said Black, "and I figured they would worship him." Another Chock executive remembers that Black had spoken of "having trouble with his employees over a trade union. He didn't want his workforce unionized. In the shops, most of the employees were black. I went to see Black in the hope that he would select Jack to take charge of personnel matters."

Robinson clearly felt the pressure. The unions "are going to attempt to discredit me in some way," he confided to a friend, "because they feel if they can intimidate me they will have a chance of getting into our shops. I feel pretty well set up defensively so I am not worried." After Chock's laborers turned down the later union-organizing vote, some filed complaints against Robinson. He had warned some black staff that a union shop would mean losing his post, said the allegers, and had claimed that "the white employees were jealous of my position in the company." The National Labor Relations Board, however, cleared him.

Unable to ever escape the racial complexities of managing his institutional power, the pressure came in two directions. Robinson feared many African American workers expected too much from him—especially in protecting them from dismissal. On the other hand, he believed that some white workers—certainly unaccustomed to ceding authority to an African American in 1950s America—resented his control over them.

Another attraction to the Chock job was Black's willingness to allow Robinson time off for his civil rights activities. With that permission, Robinson accepted the NAACP's request to lead their national "Freedom Fund Drive." Jackie had "a feeling" that he was asked "in the same spirit that many organization[s] ask public personalities to participate in their work": agreeing to lend "their names on the letterheads, attend press conferences . . . take a few publicity pictures, but let the real work be done by others." Instead, he was "determined" to be "involved as much as possible." Thus was launched his nationwide speaking tour for the civil rights organization. Needing tutoring by NAACP staff at first, Robinson emerged as an increasingly effective speaker, and he raised over $1 million (the highest mark to date for the annual Freedom Fund drive). NAACP branches commonly made the popular sports star their first choice for a speaking engagement in 1957 (before even the newly renowned Martin Luther King), and most of Robinson's weekends were spent promoting the cause.

It was not Robinson's first foray into civil rights beyond the diamond. With his life in baseball winding down, Jackie had ramped up his off-field involvement in advancing racial justice. In 1954 and 1955, he had toured the country as chairman of the Commission on Community Organizations for an early civil rights group, the National Conference of Christians and Jews (first created in 1928, it promoted religious and racial unity). In 1955, he became cochair of New York's Committee of the United Negro College Fund. He continued to speak and tour and appear on radio and television in a variety of places on the issue.

Later in 1957, Robinson apprehensively followed the Little Rock School Crisis. The Arkansas city had made an early effort to begin desegregation of its Central High School with the admission of nine African Americans. Burgeoning mobs of racist whites encircled the school, producing riot conditions and endangering the teen integrationists. Robinson publicly and privately urged President Eisenhower to intervene. When the president promoted "patience" as the drama unfolded, an angry Robinson wired him,

"We are wondering to whom you are referring when you say we must be patient." He chided those who found it "easy" to counsel forbearance when they "haven't felt the evils of a prejudiced society." Noting that he was "aware" that his "letter expresses a mood of frustration" that might unsettle the president, Robinson cautioned that it was "a mood generally found among Negro Americans today and should be a matter of concern to you as it is to us." When Eisenhower finally sent in federal paratroopers for protection, Jackie offered his "congratulations on the positive position you have taken."

The former infielder's intervention on the Little Rock crisis both indicated his growing interest in politics and his complicated role in navigating the shifting landscape of race and the two major national parties. It was a natural evolution for the civil rights pioneer, and he savvily used his entre as a popular sports star to make inroads into the world of white politics unavailable to other black leaders. Robinson, recalls his wife, had actually "used his athletics as a political forum. He never wanted to run for office, but he always wanted to influence people's thinking."

A registered Independent voter, historical context and perhaps two chance meetings shaped his early ties to the Republican Party. A far more fluid period for racial politics and the two major parties, African Americans' ties to the Democrats were well underway by the early 1950s due to Franklin Roosevelt's Depression Era poverty programs and some preliminary civil rights steps by his successor Harry Truman (including the desegregation of the military). Still, the Democrats continued to carry the taint of southern segregationists and their one-party white supremacist rule in the South. And the Republicans—who included some prominent liberals in the 1950s—had once commanded African Americans' unquestioned loyalty as the party of Abraham Lincoln. In short, blacks' party identification clearly sided with the Democrats, but a significant minority still favored the GOP.

The pro-business and ardent anticommunist Robinson (who had previously exhibited his commitment in his 1949 friendly HUAC testimony) already found common cause with the Republican Party. "Our country is engaged in a titanic struggle with a resourceful and powerful enemy," he made plain. That struggle hadn't "yet reached the shooting stage. It is now largely a struggle for men's minds." Also important to him, of course, were the parties' stance on racial issues. Though the Democrats would be known by the mid-1960s as the party much friendlier to civil rights (although never as progressive as many activists would have liked), their commitment to the cause was far from certain in the 1950s. For Robinson, the Democrats' rejection of a 1956 convention platform proposal decrying segregation was a healthy reminder that they still had a long way to go. The influence of lifelong Republican Branch Rickey (an active campaigner for GOP candidates) appears to have further solidified his political leanings.

As the years advanced, Robinson's political positions remained steady as the political winds shifted around him. His firm belief in anticommunism, promotion of business, and racial change were largely static over the years. Republicans' support of the former two issues created a mostly happy home for him, but he was eventually left behind by a GOP that proved more and more reluctant to continue its civil rights legacy as the party of Lincoln. Robinson's willingness to shift his support from one party to another later caused critics to portray him as an indecisive waffler, but the truth was that Robinson's views remained more constant than the waverings of the political parties and candidates who sought his support.

The overtures of the country's president and vice president also contributed to his political allegiance. When Dwight Eisenhower deliberately crossed the room at a 1953 Anti-Defamation League dinner to shake the sport star's hand, Robinson wrote the president that "my wife and I will always remember our experience that night. It is events like this that make us certain our faith in democracy is indeed justified." His impromptu meeting with then vice presidential candidate Richard Nixon in 1952 left an even greater impact. Both men were in Chicago during the Republican National Convention that year (Jackie simply to play the Cubs) when Nixon approached him in the hotel lobby. The candidate won quick admiration for his detailed recollections of Robinson's football exploits while at UCLA. Robinson came to view Nixon as a solid defender of civil rights, even quoting the vice president in a number of speeches. He openly supported the Republican nominees in the 1956 presidential campaign.

By 1957, however, the Republican administration had become increasingly frustrating to Robinson. Certainly the president's refusal to block the weakening of the Civil Rights Act of 1957 was a significant blow. The former Dodger wrote to White House adviser Maxwell Rabb that he was "knocked spinning" by Eisenhower's press conference urging care before passing "laws in this delicate field" that might "go too far too fast." "All over the world," Robinson cajoled, "oppressed people are crying and getting their freedom, yet in what is supposed to be the world's greatest Democracy, many of our responsible leaders appear to be unduly influenced by the few bigots who fear the universal acceptance of civil rights." Despite a more satisfactory ending, Eisenhower's foot-dragging in Little Rock only exacerbated the irritation.

His vice president, however, proved to be far more eager to please. Robinson and Richard Nixon exchanged fairly frequent correspondence, Nixon all the while trying to reassure an assertive Robinson of his seriousness on civil rights matters. Responding to Jackie's letter praising him for appearing at Ghana's new day of national independence, the politician granted that "there were a number of letters on my desk when I returned to the office today after an absence of three weeks. I can assure you, however, that there were none which meant more to me" than Robinson's. Jackie hoped to use his connection to Nixon to advance racial change, urging federal intervention in civil rights hotspots and pushing the vice president to stake out a more aggressive position on race. In June 1957, he wrote Nixon of his "deep sense of appreciation for your constant efforts to provide a greater measure of justice for Negro Americans," but lamented the "heated discussions" with friends who discovered his support of the politician. "They ask, 'How can you support Nixon after the poor civil rights record he had in the Senate? Can't you see he's making these speeches now with his eye on the presidency in 1960?' . . . I am sure you understand that I am not active in partisan politics . . . [but] a person seeking reassurance in his beliefs."

So keen was Nixon to keep Robinson in the fold that he devoted staff to send Jackie a paper compiling his civil rights record. In late 1959, as the presidential campaign approached, Robinson wrote in his newspaper column, "I've been following Nixon's career for some time now and I don't mind admitting that generally I've liked what I've seen and heard." To charges of Nixon's questionable political ethics, Robinson countered that the politician had "grown more than any other person presently in political life," including through his official visits to India and other third-world nations that had expanded his knowledge of racism. The candidate, said Robinson, could draw voters that the "Democrats consider safely in their pockets." Should the latter party select "a weak and indecisive" nominee, he "would enthusiastically support Nixon."

An additional motivation for Robinson's loyalty to the Republican candidate was his desire to force both parties to compete for the African American vote. He worried that acquiescing to the growing expectation that the Democratic Party could lay exclusive claim to black voters would put them in a weak bargaining position. As long as Democrats felt that blacks had no other safe political haven, the party could afford to ignore their demands.

Despite Robinson's relationship to the vice president, his heart and voice first went with a Democratic candidate in the 1960 campaign, Senator Hubert Humphrey. Long a favorite of the liberals, Humphrey and his record had earned the respect of many African Americans. The senator "impresses me as a being a man you can trust to do what is right by all the people," wrote Jackie to a friend. By early February, Robinson began delivering speeches on the candidate's behalf in black sections of primary cities. By May, however, John F. Kennedy's electoral successes had forced Humphrey's resignation from the race.

What followed Humphrey's withdrawal was a rigorous courting by both presumed presidential nominees (Kennedy and Nixon)—a sign of the social importance and influence of Robinson in 1960 America. This would be an undeniable challenge for the Kennedy camp. Blocking the ascension of a Kennedy presidency had been one motivating factor for Robinson to join Humphrey's forces. Despite Kennedy's later image as racially progressive, his early voting record on the matter was not promising. Jackie had always seen the Massachusetts senator as dismissive of civil rights (especially his role in attempting to slow the 1957 Civil Rights Act from passage), an image disturbingly hardened by Kennedy's publicized meeting with Alabama governor John Patterson early in the presidential campaign. Patterson, following his private breakfast meeting with Kennedy, had heartily endorsed him as "a friend of the South." Those were not encouraging words to African Americans, and they caused notable black congressman Adam Clayton Powell to conjecture that some kind of deal might have been struck with the segregationist southern Democrats.

Having already sent a prepared report celebrating his allegedly strong civil rights voting record, Kennedy felt compelled to write an open letter to Robinson defending himself once again. An unimpressed Robinson wrote a *New York Post* column shortly thereafter stating that the candidate "cannot expect any self-respecting Negro to support him with the image of Patterson . . . and [his] ilk sitting across his breakfast table. When and if Kennedy firmly and vigorously repudiates the actions and policies of this crowd, I will be happy to revaluate my position. But as long as he continues to play politics at the expense of 18,000,000 Negro Americans, then I repeat: Sen. Kennedy is not fit to be President of the U.S."

Undeterred, Kennedy made one last effort to win over the civil rights giant just before the Democratic National Convention. He arranged a meeting at the home of mutual friend Chester Bowles, a prominent Connecticut Democrat and future Kennedy administration official. It did not go well. Finding Kennedy to be "striving to please," Robinson was unnerved that he "couldn't or wouldn't look me straight in the eye." He was more shaken by a potential president "who knew little or nothing about black problems or sensibilities." Challenging his voting record, Kennedy's "manner indicated he was willing and anxious to learn, and I suppose I was being invited to be one of his teachers. Although I appreciated his truthfulness in the matter, I was appalled that he could be so ignorant of our situation and be bidding for the highest office in the land." The conversation then "almost ground to a standstill" when the senator inquired how "much would it take to get me on the bandwagon." "I don't want any of your money," Robinson replied. "'I'm just interested in helping the candidate who I think will be best for the black American.' . . . The meeting ended on that embarrassing note."

Perhaps an additional reason for Robinson's reluctance to support the Massachusetts senator was the full court press being applied by his opposition. Nixon had continued to ply the baseball legend with ingratiating correspondence throughout the late 1950s, and that only increased after Humphrey's withdrawal. When a New York state Republican official informed Nixon's secretary that Robinson "could be swung around . . . [to] the Nixon band wagon," Nixon pounced on arranging a meeting. After all, the New York official indicated, "Robinson is more or less considered sort of a god up here." Robinson emerged "more convinced than ever of his support of Nixon," and privately urged him to "not hesitate in making your own position [on racial matters] as clear to others as it was made to me." That would help overcome the still lingering "attitude some people have toward you." In fact, Robinson himself needed "answers to negative questions people constantly put to me."

The vice presidential selections only further cemented Robinson's assessment. He viewed Kennedy's choice of Texas senator Lyndon Johnson as evidence that the Democratic nominee was "a cold, calculating political machine" with "no scruples in compromising with Southern bigotry in order to insure Southern votes." While Johnson would later emerge as one of the country's most racially progressive presidents, Robinson was not alone in viewing his record at that time with considerable skepticism (including his role in watering down the 1957 Civil Rights Act) and as just another example of obstructionist southern Democrats. By contrast, Henry Cabot Lodge Jr.—who won Robinson's admiration for committing to a black cabinet officer—was Nixon's pick.

By September, Robinson was ready to throw his support publicly to Nixon. The move brought personal consequences. Both Chock Full o'Nuts and the *New York Post* put him on leave without pay as he became an active campaign participant. "A publicly owned company has no right to take sides in a political campaign," declared CEO William Black. The leave would

allow Robinson to exercise his individual voice for the campaign's remainder, claimed Black. Notably, Black (a devoted Democrat) had kept Jackie on
the payroll while he had campaigned for Humphrey. *Post* editors also indicated discomfort with a columnist who actively took part in the campaign.

Both the candidate and his campaign, however, proved a disappointment.
Robinson was discouraged by Nixon's refusal to appear in Harlem (in contrast to Kennedy) and the patronizing treatment of the vice president's few
black staff and advisers. One found "the part given me to play . . . insulting."
After repeatedly dodging press inquiries over his running mate's pledge to
appoint an African American to the cabinet, Nixon finally indicated Lodge
had spoken out of turn. Robinson began to see him now as a "consummate
political animal." Also gnawing at Jackie were the voices of many friends
who thought his support of Nixon misguided. Even his wife "was not passive," she remembers, in disagreeing with her husband over the cause. It
took the candidate's inaction on the controversial jailing of a fellow African
American finally to cause Robinson "serious doubts about Nixon."

Three weeks before the election, Martin Luther King was arrested in an
Atlanta sit-in demonstration. Brought before the bench in a suburban county
known for its Klan activity, the judge used King's violation of probation over
a prior minor traffic incident as a pretext for a four-month hard labor sentence. Shortly thereafter, the civil rights leader was hauled away in the dead
of night to a Georgia prison hundreds of miles away. This was a frightening
scenario for any African American, as some had similarly disappeared forever
in the mist of the southern "justice" system. His pregnant wife, frantic about
the fate of her husband, began calling anyone who might help. Harry Bela-
fonte, close friend and famous black entertainer, beseeched Robinson to use
his clout with Nixon staffers to intervene. "He has to call Martin right now,
today," Jackie implored campaign aide William Safire, offering up the phone
number of the jail. After a ten-minute session with Nixon himself, Robinson
emerged with "tears of frustration" recounting Nixon's fear that the call
would be "grandstanding." "Nixon doesn't deserve to win," Robinson sighed.

Compounding Nixon's inaction was the countervailing response to a
simultaneous plea received by the Kennedy camp. Coretta King had called
sympathetic Kennedy aide Harris Wofford directly about her husband's
dilemma. The candidate took immediate action, calling Coretta to express
concern, and then having his brother Robert call the judge directly to ask for
leniency. With that intercession, King secured a release, and the Democrats
secured the vast majority of the African American vote in a very tight elec-

tion. King's father, a prominent Atlanta pastor in his own right and former Nixon supporter who had misgivings about Kennedy's religion, announced that Kennedy "can be my President, Catholic or whatever he is. . . . I've got all my votes and I've got a suitcase, and I'm going up there and dump them in [Kennedy's] lap."

A deeply "disillusioned" Robinson considered pulling out of the Nixon campaign. "It's hard to explain why I stuck," he later wrote.

> It has something to do with stubbornness about continuing to believe in people even when everything indicates they are no longer worthy of support. . . . I clung to the hope that Nixon would follow through on the things he had indicated were important to him in that first meeting after the pressures of the campaign were over. . . . I admit that the Kennedy ticket had begun to look much more attractive. But I have always felt that blacks must be represented in both parties. I was fighting a last-ditch battle to keep the Republicans from becoming completely white.

A phone call with Branch Rickey also proved influential. "Mr. Rickey reassured me that Mr. Nixon was still personally the fine man I thought he was, and that I didn't want this one emotional thing to completely color my overall convictions," Robinson recounted to a reporter following the election.

Nevertheless, Jackie, feeling burned by Nixon's duplicitous assurances on racial matters, learned to take a more careful, skeptical view of future candidates. His commitment to business development and anticommunism remained, as did his determination to find a place for African American concerns in both major parties. But from this point forward, he placed civil rights at the top of his agenda in evaluating his political allegiances.

In the end, Robinson's own circuitous political path in the election stands at the center of the shifting sands of party politics in 1960 America—especially on racial matters. His understandable suspicion of Kennedy's commitment to civil rights was born partly out of the political dilemmas faced by a national Democratic figure. Kennedy struggled that year to hold together an increasingly unwieldy coalition of long-committed white southerners (who sought no change to the racial status quo) with the northern urban liberals (who were beginning to demand an end to white supremacy). Nixon's challenges illustrate the fading of the Republicans as the party of Abraham Lincoln's racial progressivism. The years ahead would bring a 1964 Barry Goldwater nomination (a strong conservative who voted against the 1964 Civil Rights Act and began to woo southern white voters to the Republican column) and a 1968 Nixon campaign that won victory on the banner of "law and order" (which some claimed to be racially coded rhetoric appealing to white voters' fears of the Black Power Movement and the rising crime rate wrought by 1960s liberal permissiveness and unruly urban blacks). One can see in the seeds of 1960s presidential politics the eventual "solid" Republican South of the coming "Reagan Revolution."

Another casualty of Nixon's campaign was Robinson's job at the *New York Post*. On the eve of the election, *Post* editor James Wechsler informed him that his column would not return following his leave during the election. The newspaper executive expressed concern that the ghostwritten nature of the column had not allowed the force of his full personality to shine "because your views and attitudes were filtered through another writer." The paper was also unhappy about Jack's "sudden appearance" in a competing newspaper during his leave. Observers did wonder whether Wechsler's vocal support of Kennedy affected his view of the value of Robinson's ideas for the notably liberal publication. A year later, Robinson returned as a columnist with the well-regarded African American paper the *New York Amsterdam News*, and he chose his first column to castigate the *Post* dismissal. "I believe the simple truth is that they became somewhat alarmed when they realized that I really meant to write what I believed. There is a peculiar parallel between some of our great Northern 'liberals' and some of our outstanding Southern liberals," he sarcastically remarked. Still smarting from the repeated criticism of his support for the Republican as an African American, he added, "They both say the same thing: 'We know the Negro and what is best for him.'"

This was, of course, not the beginning of Robinson's willingness to court controversy, and take defiant, unconventional stands. Nor would it be the end. His refusal to be contained to social expectations as a black man characterized much of his post-baseball life, where his actions proved to be as difficult to contain as he had been on the base paths. By this point in his life, he had already spurned his destiny to accept white supremacy by confronting white police as a young man, by entering the world of white college sports, even by his chafing against the limitations of Negro League baseball. As a Major Leaguer, he rejected white America's attempt to portray him as the happy black merely delighted with his white "gift" of integration. His resistance to falling easily into line as simply a partisan supporter for the Democratic Party should thus come as no surprise.

Evelyn Cunningham, later to be his personal aide, addressed the seemingly enigmatic nature of the man, and the folly of trying to box him in easily. "Jackie was not too close to many people," she relates. "He was embarrassed by adulation. On the other hand, he wanted desperately to be liked. And he knew not everyone liked him. Some people would say, 'Oh, he's a cold turkey. I don't like Jackie Robinson. He's cold.' I was never sure he liked me. To this day, I don't know for sure. But I admired him." Cunningham, however, heightens the perplexity by harkening back to what could be his very early fatherless years: "There must have been something way back in his life that had frightened him about people. I was one of the people who absolutely worshipped him, but I knew that I could only show it to him by making a joke about it. He was a very good man, but in many ways he was a sort of mystery." But the perceived cryptic nature of Robinson is no doubt magnified by his race—by the expectation that African Americans must speak and act monolithically. And that inclination can emerge both from the white community (who might be reluctant to attribute the same kind of intellectual complexity among black citizens as they might for whites) and the pressure from African American quarters to circle the wagons in ethnic solidarity against the repeated slings and arrows of white supremacy.

Late in life, he wrote about the

people who write or call or tell me in person that they are about to punish me for expressing my views. . . . As though they're talking to some school kid! Then they go on to threaten to withdraw their approval of me. One day, twenty years ago, they like the way I stole home or admired my capacity to be insulted or injured and turn and walk away. For that admiration they have given me, I am supposed henceforth and forevermore to surrender my soul. I am not allowed an opinion. If I become naturally, normally indignant, they describe my mood as one of rage. Look what we did for this guy by admiring him and here's how he repays us—by thinking he has the right to say something we don't agree with. I don't owe any living person my soul, my integrity, my freedom of thought and speech.

To put his exclamation point on the matter, he called those "who believe they have the right to restrain and repress these freedoms . . . mentally sick."

Discouraged by Nixon but unprepared to abandon a party that still shared his general views on foreign policy and business, Robinson looked for other Republicans to whom he might rally. His gaze settled on a rising star in the GOP who was a darling of northeastern liberals, New York governor Nelson Rockefeller. Robinson had become better acquainted with the governor during joint appearances in New York City's black neighborhoods in the now concluded campaign. He was further impressed with Rockefeller's civil rights credentials. His family had long been a significant contributor to black colleges, and he later revealed to Robinson that he had beseeched Nixon to intervene on King's imprisonment in a fashion similar to Jackie. Lastly, "Rocky" had won Robinson's approval for his role in placing a fairly strong civil rights plank on the 1960 Republican Party platform. Seeing in the governor a welcome, sympathetic ear, he wrote him a week after the election, "Please do not think me presumptuous because of this letter, but I can't help but feel that an effort must be made now if we are to make progress in breaking into what appears to be a solid bloc among the Negro for the Democrats."

The governor continued to impress the baseball legend in the months to come, making multiple appearances to black leaders and using his private plane to accompany Martin Luther King to a fund-raiser in the New York state capital. While there, the governor was King's prestigious companion in several additional appearances. Robinson decided to test the waters further by writing a letter to Rockefeller challenging his administration's lack of black officials. Recognizing the governor's philanthropy, Jack "wondered if Nelson Rockefeller's generosity to black causes was a compartmentalized activity of his private life." The governor then personally telephoned Robinson to set up an unpublicized meeting to discuss the matter at length. The result was a three-hour gathering including a dozen African Americans whom Robinson invited. The governor, recalled Jackie, "brought an open mind and someone to take notes" as "the people there didn't hesitate to recite harsh facts." Far more impressive to Robinson was the governor's action. Just months after the meeting, Rocky had "implemented virtually all the recommendations," including "some sweeping and drastic changes, some unprecedented appointments of blacks to high positions, ensuring influence by blacks in the governor's day-to-day policy decisions."

As Rockefeller's 1962 gubernatorial reelection approached, Robinson eagerly offered assistance, hoping that with the governor's "leadership and a determined effort" the Republicans might "erase the image [they have] among the Negro." The baseball star became a vocal advocate for Rocky's successful bid, providing entre to many African American venues. Still unafraid to buck convention, Robinson's support of the Republican for state attorney general, Louis Lefkowitz, courted considerable controversy. Lefkowitz, with Jackie's help, defeated Edward Dudley, who might have been New York's first African American to hold statewide office. Robinson responded to the strong criticism of other black leaders by portraying Lefkowitz as "one of the most dedicated, militant and conscientious public servants in the nation and who has steadily batted 1,000 percent on the civil rights issue.

Do you turn your back on him because he is a white man and you are a Negro who would like to see another Negro move up to a high office?"

Robinson's civil rights work was not confined to the halls of politics. In 1960, he was drawn to the charisma and energy of the unexpected "sit-in" movement of southern college students. Centered first in Greensboro, North Carolina, and Nashville, Tennessee, the civil rights phenomenon spread like wildfire among African American young people all over the South. Their simple practice of refusing to move from restaurants and lunch counters when denied service created a kind of chaos in segregated establishments and southern municipal governments. Later that year, the students formed an organization to capture and continue their momentum, the Student Non-violent Coordinating Committee (SNCC).

As their bail costs rose, they sought financial support. Turning away from the NAACP and Dr. King's Southern Christian Leadership Conference, which they viewed as too cautious, they instead sought out Robinson. As the civil rights fund-raiser and activist Marian Logan recounts, "SNCC got very mad because Martin [Luther King] was slow to involve himself [in aiding and supporting their efforts]. These kids who were in jail, refusing bail, finally agreed to get one guy out and sent him up North with some of them on the outside. So they came to New York. They said, 'Let's go to New York and we'll see Jackie Robinson.' He was a hero of theirs." After an informal meeting with the young crusaders, Robinson launched a quick phone fund-raising campaign that collected over $20,000 in two days. He then used his Connecticut home's considerable front lawn to stage for the students a benefit concert that drew jazz giants Ella Fitzgerald, Duke Ellington, Sarah Vaughan, and Carmen McRae. The concert would become the impetus for annual similar benefits he hosted called "Afternoons of Jazz," which continued to draw some of the best talent in the jazz community. Robinson revealed a powerful emotional connection to these students in his newspaper column. Their inspiring commitment to nonviolence "brought back memories of my own experience in breaking into major league baseball, for this was exactly the principle which Mr. Rickey and I agreed upon. . . . I can testify to the fact that it was a lot harder to turn the other cheek and refuse to fight back than it would have been to exercise a normal reaction. But it works, because sooner or later it brings a sense of shame to those who attack you. And that sense of shame is often the beginning of progress."

Robinson continued to cash in on his considerable notoriety to forward racial improvement with the 1961 Freedom Rides (a campaign of activists to desegregate interstate bus travel and terminals). When the segregationist

Figure 7.2. Robinson continued to play an active role supporting the cause of civil rights long after his baseball career had concluded. Here he appears at the 1963 March on Washington with his son David in August 1963. A signature moment for the civil rights movement, it was there that Dr. Martin Luther King delivered his famous "I Have a Dream" speech. *Source*: Library of Congress, http://www.loc.gov/pictures/item/2013648338/

Mississippi senator James Eastland tagged the Freedom Riders as communists (an often-used attack by white supremacists for civil rights activists), Robinson called his claim "ridiculous and despicable." Having well established his anticommunist credentials with his HUAC testimony and ties to the Republican Party, he turned the tables on Eastman, inquiring, "Why leave the impression with Communist Nations that the [Communist] Party has any influence in the Negro community? We have demonstrated our faith in America, and we will win our rights without the Communist." Robinson then took his fight directly to the source by writing the chair of the Interstate Commerce Commission (who held the power to order the desegregation sought by the Freedom Riders), calling it "mandatory . . . that you issue the proper directive in removing segregation and discrimination from bus transportation." Playing to Cold War fears that continuing racism would harm our ability to convince third-world nations of our moral superiority (and thus cause them to join the communist bloc), Robinson reminded him, "We are in a constant struggle for the support of the free world. It is our actions that will count, not words."

In the following year Robinson spoke to activists in Albany, Georgia, at Martin Luther King's request. While there, he visited one of the three black churches burned for their involvement in the civil rights campaign. "It really makes you want to cry deep down in your heart," he sighed to a journalist. He agreed to lead a fund-raising campaign to replace the lost structures (for which he would raise $50,000), and he left a powerful impression on those struggling for change. Wyatt Tee Walker, chief of staff to Dr. King, remembers that "Jackie Robinson had long been a hero to me, and it was like a dream come true to work with him. His presence in the South was very important to us. I have said a number of times that Jackie Robinson's entrance into the big leagues did more for race relations than all the work of the so-called forces of Christ combined. We worried about his safety in Albany and later in Birmingham, and we had a small group of people, bodyguards really, to look out for him. He was brave—he had already proven his bravery, but he showed it again in the South at a very bad time in our history."

The year 1962 was memorable for another reason: it allowed Robinson to add another accolade to his resume—Hall of Famer. The honor put him "on Cloud Nine," both as an individual achievement but more crucially as "symbolizing one of the final full acceptances of blacks in the baseball world," he later wrote. "[I]f this can happen to a guy whose parents were virtually slaves, a guy from a broken home," he celebrated, "who, in his early

years, was a delinquent, . . . then it can happen to you . . . out there who
think that life is against you." He had not taken his admission for granted,
and had "steeled myself for rejection," knowing of the potential racist objections, his combative persona, and his sometimes prickly relations with the
reporters who determined entrants. During his playing days, he marveled
that sportswriters "expected me to be grateful for what they wrote. Once a
writer came up and said I better start saying thank you if I wanted to be Most
Valuable Player. I said if I have to thank you to win MVP, I don't want the
f**king thing. And I didn't thank him, and I won it." He even penned a
column two weeks before the announcement titled "I Won't Crawl to the
Hall of Fame," insisting he left baseball with his "integrity intact . . . as a
guy who played it straight from the shoulder and from his beliefs" despite
some objections to his "'fiery temper' against violations of my personal dignity and civil rights of the people for whom I have such deep concern." The
worry may have been well founded, as he only narrowly acquired the 75
percent majority necessary.

White sportswriter Dick Young had his own misgivings about Robinson
during his playing days. Still supporting his selection to the Hall, Young
wrote just before the vote on Robinson, "He made enemies. He has a talent
for it. He has the tact of a child because he has the moral purity of a child.
When you are tactless, you make enemies. Perhaps 'enemies' is a harsh word.
I rather think that Robinson displeased people and offended them. He made
few friends among the newsmen." What would save Robinson, said Young,
was the "obvious difference between not making friends and making enemies." While an enemy "plots revenge . . . a non-friend feels indifference. I
am confident Jackie's non-friends will sweep him into the Hall of Fame"
based on real merit.

When the actual induction arrived, a clearly moved Robinson offered
thanks to three people who had been instrumental in his life: his mother,
his wife, and the "man who has been like a father to me," Branch Rickey.
Robinson subsequently wrote Rickey his regret that he had not had "you at
my side on the platform" rather than the audience. "I owe much to you," he
reminded the Deacon, "not because you brought me into baseball as the
first—but because your life has been such an inspiration to me." Robinson,
continuing to use his baseball fame for racial progress, converted his honorary dinner for the event into a fund-raiser for King's Southern Christian
Leadership Conference (SCLC) voter registration efforts. The choice rankled NAACP head Roy Wilkins, who felt that it unfairly excluded his
group's similar work (which would make fund-raising more challenging);

and, after all, the new Hall of Famer sat on the NAACP board. The kerfuffle merely highlighted Robinson's growing displeasure with Wilkins and his leadership—which he saw as cautious in policy and autocratic in style.

As the 1964 presidential race began, Robinson continued to believe deeply in the importance of African Americans having a presence and say in both political parties. "We must have a two-party system," he implored his readers. "The Negro needs to be able to occupy a bargaining position." Toward that aim, he accepted a position as a deputy director for Rockefeller's campaign for the presidency in early 1964. It meant resigning from Chock Full o'Nuts, where he had been progressively unhappy in recent years. He had complained to friends about "catching flak" for the firm's opposition to union activities and his perceived loss of influence in decision making. "I did not want to be in any job where I would be a figurehead," he later complained.

He saw his new job with the Rockefeller campaign as especially urgent—a way to ensure both the success of Rocky as well as to stave off the threat of a growing racist "counterrevolution" led by two candidates—Democrat George Wallace and Republican Barry Goldwater. Their surprising success with northern white voters left him "bitterly disappointed" in the northern electorate. Fully exposed now was the hypocrisy of northern white liberals—those who had cheered southern racial change from afar and "would much rather send a check to the NAACP, belong to some study group on race relations and observe Brotherhood Week one week out of the year." "The nation," he continued, "is in serious trouble." Americans remained concerned about external communist threats, but they were naively blind to "the creeping corruption" threatening the country as they ignored northern black ghettoes.

It was Goldwater who stood the much better chance of winning the presidency, however, and thus took the brunt of Robinson's offensive. His opposition to the Civil Rights Act of 1964 and his open courting of the white South especially raised alarm. In a 1963 piece, Jackie observed a "striking parallel" between the black separatists of Malcolm X's Nation of Islam and Goldwater supporters. "Both groups want to detour from the highway to racial integration. Both groups feel they can reach their goals by traveling the road of racial separation." The looming "danger of the Republican Party [was] being taken over by the lily-whiteist conservatives." On the stump in Oregon during the campaign, he referred to a potential party nomination for Goldwater when he warned, "If we have a bigot running for the presidency . . . it will set back the course of the country." In Minnesota, he portrayed the dangers of the election in almost apocalyptic terms: "This is a struggle to redeem the soul of America. The Negro is not interested in avenging the past, but in enriching the future. How fatal it would be if we came face to face with each other in armed camps of white versus Negro." As Goldwater built momentum during the summer months, Robinson painted him as "an advocate of white supremacy" who had "shown contempt for the Negro people."

Those concerns were grounded in part on what Robinson perceived as a disturbing rise in national racial tension. The 1963 images from Birmingham, Alabama, animated Robinson to launch a fund-raising initiative to aid King's civil rights campaign. When he and former champion boxer Floyd Patterson toured the bombing sites of King's motel and brother's home there, he remarked to a King aide, "The people who did this are animals." At a rally that evening, his voice and tenor visibly rose as he spoke to the soldiers of the struggle. "When we think about the little kids being tossed from one side of the street to the other by the tremendous force of this [fire]hose . . . this picture just sickens me, this big brave policeman down here with his knee in the throat of this lady." A few months later, he returned to the city to see the rubble of the Sixteenth Street Baptist Church, which had served as a center for the now victorious civil rights campaign. Ten to fifteen sticks of dynamite had been set to ignite during the 10 a.m. service on a Sunday morning in September. Four little girls, excitedly fixing their hair in the bathroom as they prepared themselves for their appearance in the adult choir, were killed. Robinson's friend Marian Logan recalls standing over the remains with the Hall of Famer: "I can see him standing there with his fists shaking, trying to control his fury."

Also disconcerting was what Robinson observed on the streets of the urban North. An unnerving summer race riot in Harlem broke out during the presidential election year. Lasting a week, it featured burning, looting, and fighting between blacks and the white police, and 144 injuries. Worse, the rage spread to several other northern cities that summer. "I wish I could have a heart-to-heart, man-to-man talk" with some of the young rioters, he wrote, since "their blindly reckless acts, are endangering the freedom struggle" and "playing right into the hands of the enemy." While he worried about white supremacist presidential candidates, he feared the countervailing growth of black separatism that might contribute to the emerging racial violence.

In a series of public letters and columns in 1963 and 1964 with Malcolm X, Robinson made clear his concern over the growth of black nationalism.

The two men, of course, inhabited the same geographical area but occupied very different ideological territory. Each sought to influence the emerging cadre of urban black youths who grew impatient with the cost and pace of the nonviolent civil rights movement. Robinson had harbored concern over the separatist African American organization, the Nation of Islam, and its famous minister Malcolm X for some time. In July 1963, the Hall of Famer fired off a missive in the *New York Amsterdam News* about the allegations that Malcolm's followers were responsible for the "disgraceful incident" of pelting Martin Luther King at a Harlem speaking engagement (charges denied by Malcolm X). Robinson asked if Malcolm and his nationalist adherents "want to go off into some all-black community, why don't they just go?" Since "the Negro community has demonstrated dramatically that it is opposed to separation," he even wondered whether it was really white segregationist "individuals or groups" that formed the basis of the Nation of Islam's support.

A November 1963 critique of prominent African American congressman Adam Clayton Powell Jr. for his speech criticizing African American UN official Ralph Bunche finally drew Malcolm into a heated debate. (Bunche had delivered an address denouncing Malcolm and his apparent new ally Powell as promoting "a black form of the racist virus.") In a blistering response printed on the *Amsterdam News*'s front page, Malcolm accused his opponent of being under the thumb of "white bosses" who regulated his every move, beginning with his admission into the Major Leagues. Robinson, he alleged, had allowed them to "use you to destroy Paul Robeson" at his HUAC appearance. His support of Republican candidates only continued the trend, said Malcolm.

Robinson began his published response calling the separatist leader's "attack" really "a tribute" when "coming from you. I am proud of my associations with the men you choose to call my 'white bosses.'" He applauded Rickey, Chock CEO William Black, and Rockefeller, but conspicuously did not list Nixon—as Malcolm had. Defending himself against charges of being out of touch with the black "masses"—an insinuation that must have stung as others had begun to whisper it—he sarcastically retorted, "I assume that is why NAACP branches all over the country constantly invite me to address them. I guess this is the reason the NAACP gave me its highest award . . . why Dr. Martin King has consistently invited me to participate in the Southern Freedom Fight." He urged African Americans to steer clear of Malcolm's "sick leadership." Within a few months, Malcolm's life was turned upside down by his departure from the Nation of Islam. With his time and attention drawn to trips to Africa and Mecca, and the formation of a new organization, their very public argument died down, and within a year black assassins murdered Malcolm in a New York City ballroom.

Their conflict, however, sits at the nexus of an important debate held in the African American community in the mid-1960s. And in the next several years, the inheritance of Malcolm's worldview would be the one to win more and more hearts and minds in the northern ghetto. In some ways, the definition of black manhood itself was at the heart of this change. It was clearly an issue that Robinson himself had seen evolve during his lifetime (from Jack Johnson to Joe Louis to himself), and his later years in baseball seemed to hint that he yearned to express more freely his aggression and anger.

Fascinatingly, just months after this heated debate with Malcolm, Robinson wrote a column defending the young boxer Muhammad Ali. Ali (whose recent name change from Cassius Clay, Robinson had not caught up) had just chosen Malcolm X as his trainer. "Why should I be disturbed?" Jackie asked his readers. "Clay has just as much right to ally himself" with Malcolm and the Nation of Islam "as anyone else has to be a Protestant or Catholic." He discounted worries about the "great flocks" of African Americans who might "suddenly turn to the Islam ranks." But he did caution, "If Negroes ever turn to the Black Muslim movement, in any numbers, it will not be because of Cassius or even Minister Malcolm X. It will be because white America has refused to recognize the responsible leadership of the Negro people and to grant us the same rights that any other citizen enjoys in this land."

Just as Robinson had once been a visible standard bearer for his race (and carried the passed torch for Joe Louis), Ali would soon emerge as a black athlete symbol for a different vision of black America. Though Robinson would later criticize Ali's rejection of his Vietnam War draft induction, he was not afraid to stand up for the brash young man's willingness to make his own way in defiance of white expectations. In a passage that evoked the criticism he had faced for rejecting white assumptions himself as an athlete, Robinson discussed how "the loudness—and sometimes crudeness" of the young boxer "has brought excitement back into boxing. He has spread the message that more of us need to know: 'I am the greatest,' he says. I am not advocating that Negroes think they are greater than anyone else. But I want them to know that they are just as great" as anyone else. "If we can learn to believe in ourselves one iota of the way Clay does, we'll be in great shape."

As the Republican National Convention in San Francisco approached, Robinson met Rockefeller at his Wyoming ranch. They strategized with aides on promoting the governor as the party nominee. One of only about a dozen blacks among the 1,303 delegates arriving later at the convention, Robinson found it "one of the most unforgettable and frightening experiences of my life." "The reactionary forces" and "the tactics they used to stifle their liberal opposition" left him so "appalled" that he left the convention with "a better understanding of how it must have felt to be a Jew in Hitler's Germany."

It was also Rockefeller's finest hour, thought Robinson, as the governor braved several minutes of "hysterical abuse and booing" to fight for a more liberal party and a more "enlightened attitude" toward African Americans. Initiatives to condemn the Ku Klux Klan and the John Birch Society, for example, failed to make the party platform. A plank supporting "neighborhood schools" (largely regarded as a thin attack against school desegregation) did pass. For Robinson and the paltry number of black delegates, the convention's reaction to Rockefeller's impassioned speech for the party's liberal wing was "a terrible hour" that "served notice that the party they had fought for considered them just another bunch of 'niggers.'" A southern "bigot . . . actually threw acid on a black delegate's suit jacket and burned it." African American journalist Belva Davis recalls Goldwater supporters chasing her and a black colleague from the hall, shouting, "Niggers, get out of here . . . I'm gonna kill your ass." The white delegates hurled garbage and a glass bottle "within an inch of my head." An Alabama delegate "turned on" Robinson "menacingly" as he cheered the governor. "He started up in his seat as if to come after me," Jackie recounted. "His wife grabbed his arm and pulled him back. 'Turn him loose, lady, turn him loose,' I shouted. I was ready for him. I wanted him badly, but luckily for him he obeyed his wife."

The hall, however, clearly did not want Rockefeller. Despite Goldwater's eventual drubbing in the general election as the Republican nominee, many now regard the San Francisco gathering as a key turning point for the growing power of conservatives in the party (which would come to full fruition with Ronald Reagan's 1980 victory). The convention also displayed white southerners' uncoupling from their long association with the Democrats to a Republican Party sympathetic to their objections over federal interference in racial matters. Goldwater had announced a deliberate strategy before the election of appealing to white southerners who were unsettled by the comparatively aggressive civil rights policies of Democratic president Lyndon Johnson. After Johnson put his signature to the landmark Civil Rights Act that summer, he presciently told an aide, "We have lost the South for a generation." A savvy Goldwater proposed that Republicans should now go "hunting where the ducks are." Doing just that in the general election netted a surprising four southern states for the Republican column.

When Goldwater captured the nomination, a bitter Robinson swung to support the Democratic ticket, becoming national chair of the "Republicans for Johnson Committee." So strong was his sentiment that he chastised Rockefeller for the governor's muted support of his own party's nominee: "You know and I know," he wrote, "that a Goldwater victory would result in violence and bloodshed," he wrote. Using particularly aggressive language, he contended that the governor's endorsement meant denying "the ideals and principles for which the Rockefeller name has always stood. Your doing so is one of the most disappointing things that has ever happened to me." Robinson's seeming mercurial pendulum swings between the two major parties showcases the national political shift taking place in the 1960s. His status as a liberal Republican would find a decreasingly welcome resting place in the party as the decade progressed. Likewise, conservative white southerners began to find the Democratic Party less inviting. Robinson's insistence on clinging to the ideal of a Republican Party that made room for black liberals would eventually leave him a man without political portfolio or influence.

After Johnson safely retook the White House, however, Robinson accepted a job with the Rockefeller gubernatorial administration, becoming a full political participant himself. His post actually originated with a personal letter he wrote to the governor in January 1966. Conceding that "there is not a more dedicated politician on the scene," he claimed that Rockefeller's record of African American political appointments "cannot be accepted by any self-respecting Negro. . . . Unless there is immediate action, Governor, I must publicly answer the challenges which have come to me" about his past support. Three weeks later, Robinson became Rockefeller's special assistant for community affairs, joining four other blacks on staff (including former Martin Luther King lieutenant Wyatt Tee Walker). Robinson promised at his opening press conference that "we will get around to every nook and cranny in the State. We want to talk to people. We want to try to unite as many people as we possibly can." He was eager to see, he said, "Rockefeller Republicanism triumph."

Working mostly out of the governor's Manhattan office, Robinson's responsibilities were varied, including community meetings, acting as a liaison to government agencies and committees on the governor's behalf, and public relations appearances in Rockefeller's absence. Later, Robinson transitioned into an enthusiastic campaigner for Rocky's successful 1966 reelection effort. He would write of this work as one of "most rewarding experiences of my life." In a sign of the governor's serious courting of the black vote, he launched the 1966 campaign at the Harlem offices of the black newspaper the *New York Amsterdam News*.

While Robinson's job description was rather loose, those close to the governor recognized that Robinson had earned the governor's ear. According to one staffer, the two men "went through a big love affair with one another." Their relationship (as in the case of Branch Rickey) evokes his loss of a paternal figure as a young man, and the degree to which, like Branch Rickey, he sought an almost familial relationship with the governor. If so, the sentiment appears to have been fully returned,

> They had such respect and admiration for one another, it was really like love. Rockefeller was convinced that Jackie really cared about him despite the fact that he was a rich, powerful man. [Rockefeller] wanted to be loved by everybody, but he was never certain and he would never be certain that it wasn't for his money and power. But he believed Jack. And in the meantime, he loved Jackie over and beyond his being a baseball hero. He was always puzzled and pleased that Jackie supported him and was his friend.

Another observer claimed, "[Y]ou only had to watch Rockefeller and Robinson together to know the genuine affection and respect they had for one another. It was real. Rockefeller, once he embraced you, was real. He gave you access and opportunity and contacts, and he didn't abandon you. And he embraced Jackie."

The complex relationship incongruously showed both Robinson's trademark outspokenness and his aspiration for warm relations with the mentors in his life. On the one hand, maintains Robinson's assistant in the governor's administration, Rockefeller would say, "Jackie Robinson makes me feel like a human being, because he tells me the truth—most people don't. They tell me what they think I want to hear." On the other hand, Robinson could find himself obsessing occasionally over offending his employer. The same aide recounts a harried 5:00 a.m. phone call from Jackie over a *New York Times* quote that could be read as criticizing Rockefeller. "My God, did you see the *Times?*" he anguished. When he called the governor before he arrived at his office to express his apprehension, Rockefeller simply laughed and reassured, "Jackie, I've been through so much with the press. This is not important. You and I both know there's no split between us."

Perhaps not coincidentally, his relationship with Rockefeller grew just as he was mourning the loss of "the man who had the greatest influence on my life of anyone outside my family," Branch Rickey. Robinson received the news of Rickey's fatal heart attack on his Connecticut residence telephone from New York sportswriter Phil Pepe. A long silence followed Pepe's announcement before Jackie finally uttered, "It's hard to describe how I feel. It's hard to say what is in my heart. We've always felt that Mr. Rickey was like a father to us." Pepe, clearly affected by the call, wrote the next day, "A man died in Columbia, Missouri [where Rickey expired] last night and in Stamford, Connecticut a part of another man died, too." At the funeral, a shaken Robinson confided, "He filled a void for me and I for him." Referring to the loss of Rickey's son to diabetes five years prior, he told reporters revealingly, "Here was a man who had lost a son, and myself who had never had a father."

While working for the Rockefeller administration, Robinson continued to fight for civil rights beyond the halls of politics. A project particularly important to him was the Freedom National Bank, which he opened in late 1964. The idea centered on Robinson's belief in business and economic development as key to African American improvement. The conviction had long been one of his lures to the Republican Party (which prided itself on being friendly to business interests), but it also caused him to circle back to surprising company and claims. Ostensibly more conservative civil rights organizations such as the National Urban League and the NAACP had made the push for greater employment opportunities one of their chief goals, but calls by moderate figures like Robinson for black business *ownership* actually approximated the rising claims of more radical leaders in the Freedom Movement. Robinson even lauded Malcolm X's promotion of "not only the cup of coffee but also the cup and saucer, the counter, the store, and the land on which the restaurant stood." The Hall of Famer "believed blacks ought to become producers, manufacturers, developers, and creators of businesses." "We must face the fact that we live in a very materialistic society," he wrote in a 1964 column. "Many of the social problems we have, many of the problems in the area of discrimination, are rooted in economic causes."

Toward that aim, Robinson became chairman of the board of the new Freedom National Bank in late 1964. The Harlem institution's goal was to overcome the discriminatory refusal of too many financial institutions to fund African American mortgages and businesses. This new bank, said Robinson, would function as "a community enterprise which will in every way belong to the people it is to serve." Hence, it would be owned and operated primarily by and for blacks, with stock shares in the bank first sold to local African Americans. It "adds something to [blacks'] sense of 'somebodiness,'" he boasted. "Freedom National is not just another local bank. It is symbolic of the determination of the Negro to become an integral part of the mainstream of our American economy." While the bank saw its assets grow considerably, opened two additional branches, and lasted until 1990, it was never the full success that Robinson had hoped. From the beginning it was plagued with internal conflicts over poor and questionable management, requiring the removal of two presidents in seven years.

Robinson charted the same complex and sinuous course in the 1968 presidential campaign that characterized his political allegiances earlier that decade. He began with the loyalty to a Nelson Rockefeller presidency that had defined him for several years. He maintained to the governor in late 1967 that "[e]verywhere we go, people seem to want you and do not hesitate to say so." But his greater concern was a GOP nomination for Richard Nixon or Ronald Reagan. "A nomination of either of these Goldwater men . . . will be a renewed rejection of Negro support." As he continued to urge Rocky to accept what Robinson called his "rightful role" as president, the governor's plans remained uncertain throughout much of the campaign. He was, Jackie later lamented, "off again, on again, doing what some disgusted friends and foes called a hesitation walk about his intention to seek or not to seek the 1968 nomination. There were periods when he was convinced that he ought to make a fight for the nomination and other times when he seemed resigned to the fact that his party had completely turned its back on him."

In the end, Rockefeller made a late appeal for the nomination that served as too little, too late. His failure to capture the Republican nod left Robinson "in a difficult position." In Rockefeller's absent wake was the "all-things-to-all-men phoniness" of the ascendant Richard Nixon. Having already lost the trust of Robinson long before, Nixon was now even more frightening to the Hall of Famer. He was especially unnerved that Nixon had "prostituted himself to get the Southern vote." That included reportedly awarding veto power to segregationist senator Strom Thurmond over the vice presidential selection. If true, Thurmond had used the authority well, evidenced by Nixon's choice of Spiro Agnew as his running mate. The inexperienced governor of Maryland had mostly earned fame for his sharp "law and order" rhetoric, especially aimed at the "circuit-riding, Hanoi-visiting, caterwauling, riot-inciting, burn-America-down" black figures he claimed were spawning the recent urban riots in Baltimore.

In August, Robinson resigned his post in the Rockefeller administration in anticipation of his support for Democratic Party nominee Hubert Humphrey. His departure would save Rockefeller the "embarrassing predicament of campaigning on one side of a street someday for Nixon-Agnew and having a member of his staff" across the street promoting the opposing presidential ticket. While remaining in the Republican tent for several years, Robinson had never lost touch with or faith in the sitting vice president. Now, Humphrey carried the Democratic banner and—for Jackie—the last best hope for African American voters in 1968.

The choice caused him considerable angst. In a draft of a letter to the governor, Robinson described his predicament as "perhaps the most difficult moment of my life," and expected "to return to my position with you when the campaign is over. I am aware however [of] the politics involved and can only ask if you were black and searching for dignity could you do any different?" But, now committed, the always outspoken Robinson did not mince words. In his newspaper column he continued to lament that the Republicans had been "so unsensible and so stupid" as to bypass Rockefeller to select instead "a double-talker, a two-time loser, an adjustable man with a convertible conscience—Richard Nixon. But black people do not deserve this, nor does America. The Republican Party has told the black man to go to hell. I offer them a similar invitation."

After years of charting the same hard-nosed maverick path in politics he had used on the base paths, Robinson's refusal to be pinned down as a party loyalist finally caught up with him. Following Humphrey's loss in the general election, Robinson woke up to the reality that he would not regain his job in the Rockefeller administration. While he had jumped ship politically in 1964 as well by campaigning for the Democrat Lyndon Johnson, he was not yet employed by a major Republican. This time would be too much for the governor. Robinson's aide inside the Rockefeller regime claims that Rachel Robinson was "especially bitter" over her husband's inability to return to his job. "She feels that Nelson just let Jackie down by not giving him a big appointment, a big job or something when he kind of needed one." At the same time, his long association with the Republican Party made him a suspicious commodity for many in the Democratic Party establishment.

By the late 1960s, Robinson's role and influence was shrinking not only in politics but in social and civil rights circles as well. Amid the civil rights establishment, he had angered NAACP leaders by engaging in a heated public debate with its leader Roy Wilkins in 1967. Wilkins and his lieutenants, wrote Robinson, had been running the group as "a kind of dictatorship insensitive to the trends of our times, unresponsive to the needs and aims of the Negro masses." Especially troubling was its disconnect with younger blacks who "feel the NAACP is archaic," operating out of a "'Yessir, Mr.

Charlie' point of view." A formidable opponent, Wilkins fired back somewhat tellingly. "One of these days before you are seventy, some down-to-
earth wisdom will find its way into your life. If it does nothing else except
stop you from believing that 'because I see it this way I have to say it,' it will
have done a great service. . . . If you had played ball with a hot head instead
of a cool brain, you would have remained in the minors."

Undeterred, Robinson wrote that Wilkins regretfully could not "accept
honest criticism," and then critiqued Martin Luther King later that year as
well. At issue was King's public call for an end to the war in Vietnam. With
his own son now fighting there, Robinson openly disagreed, and echoed
many civil rights moderates' unease with King's venture into foreign policy.
With so many urgent racial needs, he implored, "Let us hear from Dr. King
on the DOMESTIC crisis." Jackie also suggested it "unfair when you place
all the burden of blame upon America and none upon the Communist forces
we are fighting. . . . It strikes me that our President has made effort after
effort to convert the confrontation from the arena of battlefield to the atmosphere of conference table."

When King responded with a personal phone call, Robinson wrote a
reflective column about the "enlightening conversation." Robinson
acknowledged that he had not "changed all my opinions" on the subject,
but the minister, he proclaimed, was "still my leader . . . to whose defense I
would come at any time." Years later, in his 1972 autobiography, Jackie found
himself "more cynical about this country's role in Vietnam." He could now
look back and see that despite "how much we disagreed, I had renewed faith
in his sincerity, his capacity to make the hard, unpopular decision, and his
willingness to accept the consequences." And in a high compliment evoking
a place Robinson himself had been many times, he wrote that King "had
taken a magnificently brave and lonely stand."

The outspoken Robinson defied convention further by finding common
cause at times with young black militants. In the heat of the final months of
the 1968 presidential campaign, Robinson lifted the banner for the local
branch of the militant Black Panther Party in his newspaper column. When
members had been brutalized by local police, he favorably compared their
disciplined restraint to the future president: "Instead of taking to the streets
to retaliate, these young brothers took their complaint to City Hall where
one of the Black Panther leaders . . . bared his mutilated back to give mute
and horrible proof of the kind of brutality which would be the accepted thing
under the 'law and order' philosophy of Richard Nixon." At a follow-up
Brooklyn meeting he held with the Panthers, he suggested that he "could

have become a Black Panther as a teenager," and praised their goals as akin to mainstream civil rights organizations: "The Black Panthers seek self-determination, protection of the Black community, decent housing and employment and express opposition to police abuse."

In another controversial column, he addressed the proposed boycott of the 1968 Olympic games by black competitors. Intended to dramatize the conditions in ghettos at home, Robinson expressed "mixed emotions" about the boycott, but he clearly identified with the young men's anger. He conceded that "[m]aybe we as Negro athletes have 'been around' too long, accepting inequities and indignities and going along with the worn-out promises about how things are going to get better. If this is the way the youngsters feel, believe me, I can sympathize with their point of view." In a sign of the evolution of his racial views, he then remarkably praised even Malcolm X, with whom he had had a crackling debate earlier in the decade. "Malcolm X, the late and brilliant leader, once pointed out to me during the course of a debate that: 'Jackie, in days to come, your son and my son will not be willing to settle for things we are willing to settle for.'" (The boycott never actually materialized, but the movement did produce the stirring moment when the African American medalists in the two-hundred-meter race defiantly raised their black, leathered fists on the victory platform in solidarity with inner-city blacks back home.)

There is no doubt, however, that his role in mainstream politics poisoned young black militants' perceptions—who had to come to view cooperation with the white power structure as mere surrender to white supremacy. Late in life, he defended his role in the Rockefeller administration as not simply serving the status quo:

> When I went to the scenes of unrest and riot as the governor's representative, I went not to emphasize the "cool it" bit, but to listen and learn why things had become so hot. I didn't listen only to the law and order people or the black and white bourgeoisie. I got together the so-called militants and offered to do what I could to communicate their beefs to the governor, to housing people, and to industry. I felt the job was worthwhile and that I had made some progress for the black cause while I was in it.

Increasingly, though, jeers of "house Negro" were hurled in his direction. (The term refers to the type of African American who might have won positions in the master's house during slavery through obsequiousness.) He even received death threats from Black Power detractors. On the front steps of his Freedom National Bank in August 1968, where he publicly endorsed Hubert Humphrey, he was greeted with mostly warm applause. The major event was also interrupted, however, by shouts of "Uncle Tom!" from the Harlem crowd. "I am human," he consoled himself that year. "I like public approval as well as anyone else. But, if I have to be misunderstood and misrepresented because I follow my convictions and speak my mind, then so be it. . . . In the long run, I'm the guy I have to live with."

Tragically, as the great power he once wielded in sports, politics, and society appeared to be fading, he lost an "idol" and the nation lost "the greatest leader of the twentieth century." Slain on the balcony of a Memphis motel, Martin Luther King's death was also the catalyst for nationwide urban riots. Despite their dispute over the war, Robinson had written of the fallen leader nine months before. "If ever a man was placed on this earth by divine force to help solve the doubts and ease the hurts and dispel the fears of mortal man, I believe that man is Dr. King." In an emotional column, he recalled a 1956 sermon King had delivered to bolster blacks during the Montgomery Bus Boycott that racial reconciliation might eventually come despite continuing white violence. "Perhaps this will happen today in America," yearned Robinson. "Perhaps, after the emotions quiet down. Perhaps, after the streets of our cities are no longer haunted by angry black people seeking revenge." A month later, the darker mood that seemed to be growing in Robinson prevailed as he contemplated the nation's future without the noble influence of Dr. King. "There is no doubt in my mind that many, many whites wanted to see Dr. King silenced to death. How deeply they will regret the day."

These were not the only spreading shadows over the once muscular infielder's future. Robinson was now bereft of his political reach, unemployed, and watching the ascendancy of a new president whom he feared would usher in a reactionary era. His former aide in the governor's office remembers, "He was just floundering personally and professionally. Nothing was happening for him." Ahead, however, lay more troubles that likewise could not be conquered with athletic determination, a glove, or a bat.

CHAPTER EIGHT

Early Sunset on a Legend

> Death ain't nothing. I done seen him. Done wrassled with him. You can't tell me nothing about death. Death ain't nothing but a fastball on the outside corner. And you know what I'll do to that!. . . . You get one of them fastballs, about waist high, over the outside corner of the plate where you can get the meat of the bat on it . . . and good god! You can kiss it goodbye.
>
> —August Wilson, *Fences*

Just three days after Martin Luther King's death had rattled Robinson, he made a sobering appearance at the Stamford, Connecticut, courtroom of Judge George DiCenzo. Robinson's son, Jackie Robinson Jr., was charged with possession of heroin, marijuana, and a .22-caliber revolver. In the dark hours of early March 1968, police had interrupted a drug sale at a downtown one-night hotel. Gunshots were exchanged between the younger Robinson and police as he fled, only to be apprehended shortly thereafter. Jackie Jr. had declined his opportunity to phone his parents, and so it was that the elder Robinson found out about his son's incarceration from an Associated Press reporter who phoned him at his office. When asked for comment on his son, Robinson could only respond, "What do you mean?" It was, wrote Robinson later, "the day the roof fell in on us."

When Robinson and the rest of his shaken family arrived to post bail, he faced the inevitable scrum of reporters. Dutifully answering questions "in a whisper," observed author Roger Kahn, he appeared "a bent, gray man . . . drawing shallow breaths, because a longer breath might feed a sob." Robinson openly feared that he "had more effect on other people's kids than on my own," and he reassured that he would stand behind his son, "but we'll have to take the consequences." "God is testing me," he muttered softly.

Judge DiCenzo made those consequences comparably lenient—perhaps because the young Robinson was a first-time offender, a war veteran, and/or the son of sports legend. The defendant was given the choice of jail time or drug treatment under state supervision. Since he chose the latter, his charges would be delayed for two years. Rachel had already made arrangements for his admission to a hospital near the facility where she now worked as a nurse. When that facility proved insufficient to fully address his addictive issues, he was moved to an institution specializing in addiction, Daytop Rehabilitation. The treatment proved to be tough but productive medicine for Jackie Jr. and his parents, but the problem had been incubating for some time. The situation was also an early sign that the final years of Jackie Sr. would not be an easier journey than the hard road he had already endured.

From an early age, there had been problems with Jackie Jr. Rachel suspected that his obvious difficulties in school might have stemmed from an undiagnosed learning disability. As his educational struggles grew, the child "began to dislike school intensely," his father imparted, "and in time he earned the reputation of being a troublemaker." Jackie Jr., who showed some real athletic aptitude (his father remarked that he "could have become a major leaguer"), seemed to battle expectations as the son of a sports legend. He was not the first child of a famous person to suffer under the reality of falling short of a public parent, and he labored to find his own identity and self-assurance. Compounding the problem was surely the elder Robinson's long absences—both during his baseball career and the ample time spent touring the country for civil rights and social causes thereafter. Jackie Sr. himself admits, "Ironically, a lot of time was taken up at meetings and sports events sponsored by organizations that were in the business of helping youngsters." He came to understand after his son's troubles escalated "that I had been so busy trying to help other youngsters that I had neglected my own."

A teenage stint in boarding school ended in his expulsion, and his return home only made him appear "lost" to his parents. In early 1964, seventeen-year-old Jackie Jr. ran away with a friend, hitchhiking to California. His father, said Rachel, "just crumbled. . . . It was the first time the family . . . had seen him break down and cry. . . . [H]e was deeply, deeply hurt." There had been no precipitating argument. Instead, the boy, remembers his father, "felt that if he could be on his own for a while, he would be able to come to grips with himself." But unable to find work, he simply returned home after a two-week absence. A couple of months later, Jackie Jr. volunteered for the U.S. Army, telling his parents that "he hoped to pull himself together, get the discipline he knew he needed badly, and establish his own identity." His father brightened that "his Army stint will be a blessing" by providing him the regimen and direction so badly lacking.

To his parents' "great dismay" however, Jackie Jr. was shipped to Vietnam in the summer of 1965 amid the massive escalation of the war. In letters from the front, he wrote unnervingly of the killing of innocent women and children and how the "atrocities on our side stunned" him. One incident especially chilled him. A jeepload of American soldiers drove through a village with the body of a slain sniper tied to the hood "like a deer," warning through loudspeakers of a similar fate for any other Viet Cong. On the day after his nineteenth birthday, he narrowly escaped death, as a VC ambush took the lives of two comrades. Bearing a gunshot himself, he dragged one soldier away from the gunfire, only to see the friend expire in his arms. Despite Jackie Jr.'s responses to journalists that the incident "wasn't all that much," his parents soon learned the experience was "pretty traumatic."

After recuperating in a military hospital and a brief stint at a Colorado military base, Jackie Jr. had completed his three-year term of service. He returned home to Connecticut, said his mother, "spiritless, wounded in body and soul, cynical, afraid" and—unbeknownst to his family—a drug addict. While his father had known of his marijuana use before enlistment, it was in the army, said Jackie Jr., where he "got most heavily into drug use." That began among his military peers on base in the United States but escalated significantly after arriving in Vietnam. "I used drugs constantly for the remaining two years of my tour of duty, including pills and opium," he later testified. And he was not alone; by his own estimation, "about 25 percent of my outfit" used at least marijuana (often dipped in opium) daily, and upward of 75 percent imbibed "irregularly."

The alarming drug use was brought on by the wide availability and greater potency of drugs in that region (especially of opium-based narcotics like heroin), soldiers' growing unease over some of the apparent unethical U.S. military conduct, as well as the common anxiety in any war that—in Jackie Jr.'s words—"the next hour or the next day you are going to be going back out and facing the people who are hostile and want to kill you." (By 1970, U.S. brass in Saigon itself confidentially estimated that sixty-five thousand American servicemen were on drugs, with one helicopter pilot claiming the "majority of [soldiers] were high all the time.") Whatever the reason, the result was that American soldiers were sometimes high when responding to villagers and combat conditions. Jackie Jr. was not the only soldier to worry that the unsettling numbers of "'accidental' deaths were possibly caused by some GI's" suffering from amplified anxiety due to drug use.

It was after his discharge and return to Connecticut that Jackie Jr.'s life really spiraled out of control. His mother noticed that he "seemed to want to walk as close to the buildings as possible, almost hugging them. He told me that this was Vietnam taking over; he was keeping close to cover." He drifted from the family home, consorting with pushers, prostitutes, and all manner of street criminals. He even interacted with local mafia figures. He "knew about Mafia contracts, about murdering people," his father later confided to a writer. Sometimes living on the street, he began breaking into homes and selling drugs to support his habit.

His March 1968 arrest halted this dangerous descent and finally brought him to a treatment program. After a few months at Daytop Rehabilitation, however, he had escaped and was arrested again in a Stamford hotel with a nineteen-year-old woman and charged with "using females for immoral purposes" (a charge commonly used against a suspected pimp). According to police reports, the young Robinson had even frighteningly pointed his gun at arriving officers but somehow escaped unscathed. Again, the judge was lenient, ordering him back to the rehab facility and delivering a two-to-four-year suspended sentence. After a few more minor relapses along the way, Jackie Jr. graduated from the Daytop program in late 1970 and seemed to be on his way to a healthy future.

The truth, of course, was that Robinson's son had fallen prey to the same issues that troubled many young men of his era. The dilemmas of the war and drugs swept far too many families—especially African American families—up in the whirlwind of the late 1960s. Poignantly, Robinson devoted considerable energy in those years to community agencies assisting young black males with the very demons that afflicted his own son. Further weighing on his mind must have been his struggle to be fully the father figure he lacked in his own youth. He wrote in a 1967 column in words that can be easily read with an autobiographical eye: "As I look around today and observe how lost and frustrated and bitter our youngsters are, I find myself wishing that there was some way to reach out to them and let them know that we want to try to understand their problems; that we want to help. I confess I don't know the way."

If Jackie Jr.'s health appeared finally on course, one could not say the same for Jackie Robinson Sr.'s physical condition. In his first year out of baseball, he had been diagnosed as diabetic, a condition that had apparently advanced without treatment for some time and contributed to a number of other debilitating maladies. In early 1963, a procedure to repair his knee spiraled into a two-week hospital experience slipping in and out of consciousness, and caused an alarming spike of diabetic complications. An infection had set in following the surgery, and a frightened Rachel remembers that the "poison [in his system from the infection] was systemic, and it wasn't clear right away that the antibiotics would work in time." Shaken by the incident, he spoke frankly of being "deeply concerned" that he might have been "taken away."

By 1964, close friends grew concerned about his obvious physical decline, marked by his full shock of gray hair at age forty-five and his slow walk aided by a cane. In 1965, he suffered a heart attack, which tempered him further. Doctors had begun warning him to slow down, but his civil rights and political activities continued apace. When he almost collapsed out in public three years later, doctors determined he had suffered another mild heart attack.

His diabetes was playing havoc with his circulatory system and beginning to harm his eyesight. But no one can ignore the terrific toll the burden of breaking baseball's color barrier had taken on the fading giant. Overhearing her husband downplay yet again that price in an interview in the last year of his life, she leaned in to caution the journalist, "Remember, don't let him fool you. When I hear him talk about it to others, it always seems less devastating than it was." Hall of Famer Monte Irvin, one of the lucky Negro Leaguers to play several years in the Majors, recalled Robinson endured constant "stomach pains" while playing in the Major Leagues, which he kept to himself. "Maybe they were psychosomatic or maybe he was so full of nervous tension, but he always had that pain in his gut and look what he was able to do despite it." Evidence of the malady's source, says Irvin, came when he retired from the game and "his pains disappeared."

Still, he soldiered on, no doubt knowing his years would be limited. Looking for a job to replace his lost position with state government, Robinson became a promoter for Sea Host, a fast food seafood chain. Capitalizing on his sports fame, Robinson would draw attention to the restaurant on radio and television. Returning to his aspiration of spurring black business ownership, he hoped that the low cost of owning a Sea Host franchise would provide a springboard for enterprising African Americans to climb the socioeconomic ladder. "Our aim," he trumpeted, "is to help people help themselves. With the company's training program and support, almost anyone prepared to work for his income can become a successful Sea Host franchisee." But Robinson ran head on yet again with minorities' limited capital when they had difficulty raising the funds even for the low-bar cost of a Sea Host franchise. He thus established Jackie Robinson Associates, which acquired monies from the Ford Foundation to loan prospective minority business owners. "We don't want the company to own stores in the black and Puerto Rican areas," he said. "We want blacks and Puerto Ricans to own these stores." Sea Host, however, was never as successful as hoped, and was bankrupt by late 1970.

A business project yet closer to Robinson's heart was launched in early 1970. Robinson used his still-notable name to recruit the interest and financial backing of three white real estate entrepreneurs to begin the Jackie Robinson Construction Corporation. While he hoped the company would provide him with an income to support his family, his main goal was philanthropic. "The single most important thing for the black community is decent housing," he told journalist Roger Kahn. "Integrate the schools, improve the schools, but still if kids don't have a decent home to go back to, they'll hit the streets. So that's where I start." Still troubled by the dangerous disregard for inner-city black youth in the late 1960s and early 1970s, he cited Brooklyn "as a characteristic place with a troubled inner city. There are thousands and thousands of fine homes there, the old brownstones from the 19th century. But they're falling apart. Decaying. Roaches. Rats. Bad wiring. I'm starting a company that's going to remodel these old buildings. Fix them up. Clean them up." More than that, he remained committed to black enterprise and economic improvement. "We're going to use black workers. So here's what we'll be doing. Providing livable housing for the black community. Providing decent jobs within the black community." One of Robinson's white financial backers elaborated that the corporation "would be a truly interracial company dedicated to training contractors who had never worked on big projects." More successful than many of Robinson's business ventures, the company would come to construct roughly 1,600 housing units, as well as provide many desperately needed jobs to the surrounding community.

In the summer of 1969, Robinson began to prepare to write his last book, an autobiography titled *I Never Had It Made.* Approaching Random House publishing, he met with a bright, young, black female editor, whose first novel was soon to appear. Toni Morrison would later be considered one of the great American writers of her generation, but now she was a book editor eager to expand the old publisher's catalog to include more black authors. After an initial meeting with the Hall of Famer, Morrison was "very enthusiastic" and saw him as "such a fascinating person." She next took him to meet her white male superiors to finalize a deal. The conversation went well at first as Jack regaled the men with baseball exploits, but Morrison saw the encounter turn when he steered away from sports—a more comfortable terrain for his white audience. He revealed that "he wanted his book to be about more than baseball. He wanted it to be about the larger picture, about society and the times he had lived through." It was then she saw "the interest ebbing from the room. The white men became cool, indifferent. They wanted something more exotic, something more voluptuous than he was prepared to offer."

A disappointed Robinson took the project to Putnam instead, but it was just one more sign of his growing inability to influence the world around him that he had once turned on its ear in 1947. For Black Power activists, the static impression of the baseball player who had refused to strike back made him seem far too timid and ineffectual for the tenor of the times. A 1969 column he wrote about a dispute with his daughter seemed to highlight the generational divide. Seeing a poster of Eldridge Cleaver hanging in her bedroom, Robinson insisted she take it down. "I object to our young people having heroes who have been involved with dope, or who have gone to prison. Let's not look up to guys because they make a lot of noise," he pleaded. Instead, he offered National Urban League president Whitney Young as an admirable substitute. Known as a civil rights moderate who worked within the system for greater job opportunities and friendlier government policies for African Americans, Robinson instructed readers that Young "has done more than all the Eldridge Cleavers . . . in terms of bettering our position. You know, if a guy goes out and shoots and kills a police officer, in too many areas he's a hero. Too many of our young people don't care whether or not a guy has committed a crime."

Lost on the young militants, of course, was the original boldness of Robinson's challenge to white supremacy before they were born. While much aggressive rhetoric filled the air in black ghettos of the late 1960s, few could have matched the courage of the Dodgers' lone black player regularly running onto a field aware that somewhere in the stands might be a white supremacist intending to make good on the latest death threat.

As he had done so often in the past, Robinson also continued to defy categories in his final years. To those African Americans who saw him as anachronistic moderate, his bleak assessment of the nation's direction said otherwise. Nixon's administration had proven to be largely what Robinson had warned of in the campaign, and his faith in the possibility of a comfortable home for blacks in the Republican Party now grew more and more bitterly distant. So unnerved had he become by white conservatives' jingoistic celebration of "law and order" that he told a reporter, "I wouldn't fly the flag on the Fourth of July or any other day. When I see a car with a flag pasted on it I figure the guy behind the wheel isn't my friend." Nelson Rockefeller also proved a disappointment to Robinson in his final few years. Observing the governor's "slashes" to welfare and education funding, Robinson worried that Rockefeller had made "a sharp right turn away from the stand of the man who once fought the Old Guard Republican Establishment so courageously." At a summer 1971 meeting Robinson challenged the politician so strongly that "[f]or the first time he became a little angry with me." Nevertheless, Robinson claimed their "warm personal relationship still exists."

More troubling was the incident a few months after their meeting in a prison in upstate New York. Inmates, angry over officials' refusal to address a variety of reforms, rebelled and seized Attica Prison and over two-dozen guards. A four-day standoff ensued as the black prisoners demanded an audience with the governor. Rockefeller defended his refusal by saying, "There was the whole rule of law to consider, the whole fabric of our society, in fact." Instead, the governor ordered a massive assault on the institution that produced forty-two deaths (including ten correctional officers). Against the backdrop of the law-and-order rhetoric, one triumphant guard called it "the swiftest and most skillful revolutionary offensive since the 1968 Tet attack in South Vietnam." The episode meant that Robinson was "under constant fire" from friends and family who were appalled at Rockefeller's role in the tragedy.

For those whose view of Robinson might still be frozen by their 1947 impressions of a compliant player just happy to be in the white world of the Major Leagues, his remarks in this period were a clear rejoinder. "I want to warn the white world that young blacks today are not willing—nor should they be—to endure the humiliations I did," he wrote in his autobiography. He went on to find common cause with a militant figure with whom he had clashed earlier—Malcolm X. Noting those earlier disagreements with the black separatist, he

> certainly agreed with him when he said, "Don't tell me about progress the black man has made. You don't stick a knife ten inches in my back, pull it out three or four, then tell me I'm making progress." . . . Whites are expert game-players in their contests to maintain absolute power. One of their time-honored gimmicks is to point to individual blacks who have achieved recognition. . . . As one of those who has "made it," I would like to be thought of as an inspiration to our young. But I don't want them lied to. . . . If a black becomes too important or too big for his racial britches or if he has too much power, he will get cut down.

He continued to oppose "complete [racial] separatism," but sounded again surprisingly receptive to the new black militants when seeing "a valid necessity for blacks to stand apart and develop themselves independently. We must have a sense of our own identity and we must develop an economic unity so we can build an independent power base from which to deal with whites on a more equal basis." Trumpeting his Freedom National Bank as a good vehicle for that principle, he asserted, "It is only through such accomplishments as these that we can negotiate from strength and self-respect rather than from the weak position of trying to be included in already existing white institutions."

Jackie Robinson's physical condition continued a steep decline. After a physical exam in the fall of 1969, the doctor took Rachel aside to warn that her husband had only two or three years left to live. Several months later, he suffered two mild strokes, hampering his balance and further attacking his vision. Struggling with severe hypertension, fatigue, and shortness of breath, he endured two hospital stays in 1970.

A greater affliction awaited in the summer of 1971. Awakened by a state trooper in the early morning, Robinson was told that Jackie Jr. had died in an auto accident. Apparently falling asleep at the wheel, his sports car had careened off a cliff, breaking his neck. After finally graduating from the rehab facility, Jackie Jr. had become an assistant director there as his life seemed set on the right path. Now he was gone. His father could only remember going "weak all over" as his other son, David, volunteered to "take that awful responsibility" of identifying the corpse. Jackie Sr. "knew that I couldn't go to that hospital . . . and look at my dead son's body." An arriving close friend recalled it as "the first time I ever saw him break in my life." The Brooklyn funeral brought out 1,500 people to pay their last respects. Still, the increasingly weakened Robinson carried on.

Consoling himself with the successes of his other two children (David had enrolled at Stanford, and Sharon entered nursing school happily married), his health nevertheless declined precipitously. Only fifty-two years old, his body bore the strain and scars of a man far older. Rachel now admits that there was a "shadow hovering over us. . . . It was like being in a race . . . a race with death." In June 1972, he traveled to Los Angeles for the Dodgers' retirement of his jersey number (the Dodgers had relocated from their Brooklyn home to Los Angeles in 1958). The event was made possible by the death of Walter O'Malley, whose friction with Robinson grew into a lifelong grudge at the controversy over Robinson's 1957 retirement. The Dodgers owner's son, Peter O'Malley, issued the invitation to heal old wounds, and Robinson called the occasion "truly one of the greatest moments of my life." More sobering was the visage of the man who shuffled onto the field to accept the honor. "He walked," said sportswriter Doc Young, "like a man of 80." Now functionally blind, a ball tossed softly underhand hit him in the head, jarring his Dodgers cap. "Oh, it was sad!" regretted Young. A close friend saw Robinson as "forcing himself to keep going; he had too much determination to stop. I just felt bad, real bad. I can't even describe it." Robinson was told the diabetes had so limited his legs' blood supply that he should prepare for their amputation.

In October 1972, Jackie Robinson's once mighty body finally gave way. Preparing for a doctor's visit, a massive heart attack took him down. The funeral brought out numerous dignitaries: civil rights leaders from Roy Wilkins to A. Philip Randolph, sports stars from Henry Aaron to Roy Campanella, and political figures from Sargent Shriver to Nelson Rockefeller. Jesse Jackson, the rising black leader with whom the Robinson family had established a warm relationship, delivered the eulogy, calling Robinson "a balm in Gilead, in America, in Ebbets Field." The hearse then proceeded through Harlem as crowds lined the streets, pausing along the way in front of Freedom National Bank and the blighted section of Bedford-Stuyvesant where the Jackie Robinson Construction Company had recently broken ground.

Not surprisingly, the tributes poured in. President Nixon, the object of much recent criticism by the deceased, still heralded the "new human dimension" Robinson had brought "to every area of American life where black and white people work side by side." *New York Times* columnist Red Smith claimed that the "word for Jackie Robinson is 'unconquerable.' . . . He would not be defeated. Not by the other team and not by life." Robinson's idol Joe Louis contributed his own admiration in an interview that Robinson would have especially appreciated. "Jackie is my hero," he told a reporter. "He don't bite his tongue for nothing. I just don't have the guts, you might call it, to say what he says. . . . But he talks the way he feels." Journalist Roger Kahn put it more simply in a 1996 article: "He lived his ideals. He was himself an ambulatory ideal."

Most telling, though, of Robinson's impact would not be the famous names who cited him, nor even the lesser sports figures that found inspiration in his courage and endurance. Just before his death, as his mounting physical maladies began to be publicized, an African American woman in Detroit, who surely had very little financial resources, made another offer in gratitude for the life lived by the Dodger great. By telegram, she beseeched the editor of the *New York Times*, "I am trying to get in touch with Jackie Robinson that once played with the Brooklyn Dodgers. Will you please print this and whatever it costs send me the bill and I'll pay you. 'Jackie I read in the *Free Press* this morning that you've lost sight in your right eye and is very bad in the left. Do you think a transplant will help? I will be glad to give you one of mine. You can call me at work between 8:15 and 5:30 PM.'"

By then, perhaps, his vision had understandably succumbed not just to the side effects of diabetes but also to the strain of all that he had seen in his short fifty-three years: the strain of seeing beyond Jim Crow limitations to a place for a young black man in America, white Major Leaguers' pitches directed at his head, snarled racists at the 1964 Republican convention when he had hoped to make blacks welcome in more corners of American politics, the depressing television images of the late 1960s as hopes for real racial changes seemed to be unraveling. What he had seen had no doubt taken its toll. This anonymous black woman understood better than anyone else how he might need new eyes.

Afterword

Jackie Robinson's legacy runs far beyond his funeral cortege. Perhaps most immediately, he left an indelible mark on athletics and the African Americans who would seek to enter them for generations to come. Just before his death, *Sport* magazine feted Robinson as the most "significant athlete" of the past quarter century. Delivering an appreciation, black basketball legend Bill Russell acknowledged that he rarely attended such banquets but made a notable exception for Robinson. "I never saw him play ball," Russell conceded. "But I would go halfway around the world to honor him because he was and is a man." Kareem Abdul-Jabbar, whom two Hall of Fame peers named the greatest basketball player who ever lived, wrote this poignant diary entry on his birthday during his final season in 1989:

> My thoughts are on Jackie Robinson today, my birthday. I was born in Harlem the day after Jackie's first major league game across the river in Brooklyn's Ebbets Field. It was forty-two years ago that I was born and that Jackie Robinson, in 1947, at age twenty-eight, crossed baseball's color line. I have always considered it a gift that I slipped into the world just at that moment. All the courage and competitiveness of Jackie Robinson affects me to this day. If I patterned my life after anyone, it was him.

Hank Aaron (who followed Robinson into the Majors from the Negro Leagues by twenty years) would have to brave racist abuse on his way to conquering the revered Babe Ruth's long-standing home run record in 1974. He maintained that he "never dreamed of the big leagues until Jackie broke in with the Dodgers in 1947." Robinson, he contended, was "the Dr. King of baseball."

157

But the greater meaning of Robinson's life, of course, is how he used a bat and glove to battle the racial fears and barriers of his day. Rachel Robinson recalls that when her husband first took a Major League field, "the meaning of the moment for me seemed to transcend the winning of a ballgame. The possibility of social change seemed more concrete, and the need for it seemed more imperative. I believe that the single most important impact of Jack's presence was that it enabled white baseball fans to root for a black man, thus encouraging more whites to realize that all our destinies were inextricably linked." Sportswriter Leonard Koppett claims that Robinson's arrival "compelled millions of decent white people to confront the fact of race prejudice—a fact they had been able to ignore for generations before. The consequences of the waves his appearance made [in baseball games across the country] spread far beyond baseball . . . to the very substance of a culture."

Author Roger Kahn recalls how Robinson's teammates

> marched unevenly against the sin of bigotry. That spirit leaped from the field into the surrounding two-tiered grandstand. A man felt it; it became part of him, quite painlessly. . . . Below, Robinson lines a double into the left-field corner. He steals third. . . . That colored guy's got balls, I tell you that. By applauding Robinson, a man did not feel that he was taking a stand on school integration, or on open housing. But for an instant he had accepted Robinson simply as a hometown ball player. To disregard color, even for an instant, is to step away from the old prejudices, the old hatred. That is not a path on which many double back. . . . Everywhere, in New England drawing rooms and on porches in the South, in California, which had no major league baseball teams and in New York City, which had three, men and women talked about the Jackie Robinson Dodgers, and as they talked they confronted themselves and American racism. That confrontation was, I believe, as important as *Brown vs. Board of Education of Topeka*, in creating the racially troubled hopeful present.

That story played itself out in very personal ways, such as Dodgers radio announcer Red Barber. Born and raised in the South, Rickey's advance warning to Barber that a black player was coming to the Dodgers left him "shaken . . . to my heels." He returned home telling his wife that he must quit his job, as he could not stomach the thought of announcing an integrated team. "It tortured me," Barber recounted. But after some agonizing reflection, he arrived at the conclusion that "[a]ll I had to do was treat him as a man, a fellow man, treat him as a ballplayer, broadcast the ball." That alone—the very act of seeking simple neutrality on Robinson's race—was life altering. And without Robinson's arrival forcing the issue, Barber might have gone many years longer not confronting the racial skeletons rattling in his closet. But arrive Robinson did, carrying the weight of a race with him, and compelling Barber to "do a deep self-examination. I attempted to find out who I was. I know that if I have achieved any understanding and tolerance in my life . . . it all stems from this." Those reformed convictions were passed on to his daughter, who was to volunteer as a teacher of young black children in Harlem.

The very fact of Robinson's presence itself became an early harbinger of the racial change that lay ahead. As Branch Rickey put it, "Integration in baseball started public integration on trains, in Pullmans, in dining cars, in restaurants in the South, long before the issue of public accommodations became daily news." Even Roy Campanella—not known as a civil rights crusader—came to claim, "All I know is that the ball clubs going down [to the South] and playing together, and traveling together, and then eating together and all, we were the first every time; we were like the teachers of it." Teammate Don Newcombe went further: "We were paying our dues long before the civil rights marches. Martin Luther King told me, in my home one night, 'You'll never know what you and Jackie and Roy did to make it possible to do my job.'" King once confided to close aide Wyatt Tee Walker that without Robinson, "I would never have been able to do what I did."

One notable difference between Robinson and his famous athletic forerunners, Joe Louis and Jesse Owens, was that Robinson's arrival came in the midst of a team (rather than the individually oriented achievements of boxing and track). While entering a team sport forced Robinson into the uncomfortable terrain of the repeated encounters with reluctant whites and "their" locker room, it also came to symbolize more powerfully the broader societal integration of the 1950s and 1960s. Robinson's daily interactions on the diamond stood metaphorically for American society in a quite visible and public way. The collective nature of baseball thus allowed some whites to imagine white players as stand-ins for the more receptive whites in American society, who heroically made possible the project of integration.

In 2005, the Class A Brooklyn Cyclones baseball club unveiled a statue of two men, side by side, one black and one white. They stand simply enough, in Brooklyn Dodgers uniforms, the white player draping his arm around the black. It is meant to depict a now famous, decidedly human, moment in the story of Jackie Robinson. Amid white fans' racist taunts during Jackie's first year in the Major Leagues, Dodgers shortstop Pee Wee Reese sauntered over to his African American teammate and put his arm around him, silencing the crowd. The gesture, remembered so fondly to this day, spoke volumes. It said Robinson and his fellow blacks are here to stay. It said I, a white man, stand with this black man. It said, of course, "we" are all on the same team after all. In his later years, Reese could only say of the moment, "Something in my gut reacted at the moment. Something about what? The unfairness of it? The injustice of it? I don't know."

All the more remarkable was that Reese's background clearly inclined him against reaching out to Robinson. The son of a railroad detective, he grew up in Kentucky and learned his white supremacist lessons early, from both family and friends. Neighborhood children frequently hurled rocks and racist barbs at African American children. "In the park that I grew up in, there were no blacks allowed," he remembered. "Blacks got in the back of the buses, they had a special fountain to drink from. I don't guess that I ever shook the hand of a black person." He heard of Jackie's signing on a naval vessel near Guam, returning from three years at war in the Pacific. His reluctance at embracing Branch Rickey's "great experiment" of integration was tempered by his eagerness to return at all costs to the game he loved. The latter was no doubt an important factor in his decision to be one of the only three southern Dodgers to decline signing the aborted 1947 player petition (which demanded Robinson not be allowed on the team).

Over time, Robinson's noble example began to win over the Kentuckian. He admitted viewing Jackie in the first couple of years in the Majors as simply "a big black guy who came into a white man's game." Later, he "started to appreciate him when I put myself into his shoes—a white player trying to break into a black league. No way I could have done it." "My father had done his own soul searching," maintains son Mark Reese, "and he knew that some fans, teammates, and yes, some family members didn't want him to play with a black man. But, my father listened to his heart, and not to the chorus."

Rachel Robinson recalled the impact of Reese's famous embrace on her beleaguered husband. "I remember Jackie talking about Pee Wee's gesture the day it happened. It came as such a relief to him, that a teammate and the captain of the team would go out of his way in such a public fashion to express friendship." In the seasons that followed, Reese and Robinson grew in that friendship, Reese telling his teammate that "I wasn't trying to be the great white father. We became very close friends. . . . He was just a fine individual, one of the greatest competitors I've ever seen."

On the day of the statue's dedication, Rachel celebrated it as "a historic symbol of a wonderful legacy of friendship, of teamwork, of courage—of a lot of things we hope we will be able to pass on to young people. And we hope they will be motivated by it, be inspired by it and think about what it would be like to stand up, dare to challenge the status quo and find a friend there who will come over and support you." Brooklyn borough president Marty Markowitz, one of a number of local luminaries present, proclaimed, "When Pee Wee Reese threw his arm around Jackie Robinson's shoulder in this legendary gesture of support and friendship, they showed America and the world that racial discrimination is unacceptable and un-American."

A powerful moment indeed—except a close examination of the record reveals considerable questions about its occurrence. The event is traditionally celebrated as happening at a 1947 game in Cincinnati—just across the river from Reese's Kentucky home. Journalist Lester Rodney, for example, vividly recounts years later that "Pee Wee dropped his glove at shortstop and walked over. I was there that day. That kind of drama, how do you measure it?" The only trouble is that Rodney never included the remarkable "drama" in his own newspaper accounts of the Cincinnati series. Neither did anyone else. There was no contemporary account whatsoever—even in the far more descriptive black newspaper stories—to pin it down as happening. That includes Robinson, who included no such story in his 1948 autobiography. The *Sporting News* wrote a 1956 piece claiming it took place before the 1947 season even got underway, during a Fort Worth exhibition game. Others remember it happening in Boston later that year. Some accounts place it during pregame warmups, or in midgame after a Robinson fielding error.

It was not until 1949 that Robinson first discussed the moment, but mentioned no physical contact. Reese, he told a reporter, "kind of sensed the sort of hopeless, dead feeling in me" and then modestly "came over and stood beside me for a while. . . . I will never forget it." By 1952, Robinson dated it as 1948 in Boston, which he later cemented with his 1960 autobiography (and came to include the addition of the arm across the shoulders). Others date it in 1948 as well. Carl Erskine, who did not join the team until 1948, claims to have been there. That later year seems more likely, particularly as written versions of the first season by both Robinson and Rickey do not discuss Reese as an especially vocal ally of Robinson. That would come later.

The year is significant. A public embrace of Robinson during his tumultuous first season in the Majors—when the questions of his legitimacy and endurance were especially scrutinized—would have been far more meaningful than a later season.

To his credit, though, Reese has never tried to promote himself as the protagonist of the story. In an interview on the fiftieth anniversary of Robinson's first Major League game, the seventy-eight-year-old Reese cautioned, "Just don't make me out to be a hero. It took no courage to do what I did. Jackie had the courage. If it had been me, a white man, trying to be the only one in the black leagues, I couldn't have done it. What he had to endure, the criticism, the catcalls—I wouldn't have had the courage." On the day of the statue's unveiling, his widow maintained that he "thought nothing of it. For him, it was a simple gesture of friendship. He had no idea that it would become so significant. He would be absolutely amazed."

Other whites' memories of Reese's action have become another matter, and serve as powerful markers for American whites who would like to forget their troubled racial past. Just as white southerners now commonly deny participating in the white supremacist resistance to the civil rights movement, white memories of Robinson's sacrifices have inevitably been sanitized into a story of whites warmly welcoming him to the heart of American society. If Reese played a helpful role for Robinson, it certainly appears to have come later and been less common than we would like to recall. But our rosier recollection of Robinson's sacrifices is just as frozen as the statue that stands at the entry to the Cyclones' field. And that is just one more burden borne by Jackie Robinson.

Bibliographic Essay

Of the existing biographies of Robinson, two are the best: Arnold Rampersad, *Jackie Robinson: A Biography* (New York: Knopf, 1997) and Jules Tygiel, *Baseball's Great Experiment: Jackie Robinson and His Legacy*, expanded edition (New York: Oxford University Press, 1997). Tygiel has also supplemented that book's significant contribution by producing two important collections: Jules Tygiel, ed., *The Jackie Robinson Reader: Perspectives on an American Hero* (New York: Dutton, 1997) and Jules Tygiel, *Extra Bases: Reflections on Jackie Robinson, Race, and Baseball History* (Lincoln: University of Nebraska Press, 2002). David Falkner, *Great Time Coming: The Life of Jackie Robinson from Baseball to Birmingham* (New York: Simon and Schuster, 1995), is another source.

Michael G. Long has issued two edited collections on Robinson: *First Class Citizenship: The Civil Rights Letters of Jackie Robinson* (New York: Times Books, 2007) and a collection of Robinson's newspaper columns on a variety of subjects, *Beyond Home Plate: Jackie Robinson on Life after Baseball* (Syracuse, NY: Syracuse University Press, 2013). Another is Joseph Dorinson and Joram Warmund, eds., *Jackie Robinson: Race, Sports, and the American Dream* (Armonk, NY: M. E. Sharpe, 1998).

Robinson and his family have produced several autobiographies: Carl Rowan with Jackie Robinson, *Wait Till Next Year: The Story of Jackie Robinson* (New York: Random House, 1960), Jackie Robinson, *Baseball Has Done It* (Philadelphia: J. B. Lippincott Company, 1964), and Jackie Robinson as told to Alfred Duckett, *I Never Had It Made: An Autobiography of Jackie Robinson* (New York: Putnam, 1972). Sharon Robinson published *Stealing Home: An*

Intimate Family Portrait by the Daughter of Jackie Robinson (New York: Harper Collins, 1996), and his wife, Rachel Robinson, wrote with Lee Daniels *Jackie Robinson: An Intimate Portrait* (New York: Harry N. Abrams Publishers, 1996).

Chapters 1 and 2

Besides Robinson's court martial records, Truman Gibson (with Steve Hunt-ley) provides his own account of African American struggles during World War II from inside the presidential administration in his *Knocking Down Barriers: My Fight for Black America* (Evanston, IL: Northwestern University Press, 2005). Further background on the racial context for World War II can be found in John Morton Blum, *V Was for Victory: Politics and American Culture during World War II* (New York: Harcourt Brace, 1976); Paula Pfeffer, *A. Philip Randolph, Pioneer of the Civil Rights Movement* (Baton Rouge: Louisiana State University Press, 1990); Ronald Takaki, *Double Victory: A Multicultural History of America in World War II* (Boston: Little, Brown, and Company, 2000); and Richard Dalfiume, "The Forgotten Years of the Negro Revolution," *Journal of American History* 55 (June 1968): 90–106. Also helpful on the war are Michael C. C. Adams, *The Best War Ever: America and World War II* (Baltimore: Johns Hopkins University Press, 1994); John W. Dower, *War without Mercy: Race and Power in the Pacific War* (New York: Pantheon, 1986); and David M. Kennedy, *Freedom from Fear: The American People in Depression and War, 1929–1945* (New York: Oxford University Press, 1999). For more specific coverage on Robinson's region during the period, see Josh Sides, *L.A. City Limits: African American Los Angeles from the Great Depression to the Present* (Berkeley: University of California Press, 2003).

Sources on Joe Louis include Chris Mead, *Champion Joe Louis: A Biography* (London: Robson Books, 1993); Lauren Rebecca Sklaroff, "Constructing G.I. Joe Louis: Cultural Solutions to the 'Negro Problem' during World War II," *Journal of American History* 89, no. 3 (December 2002): 958–83; Gerald Astor, "*. . . And a Credit to His Race": The Hard Life and Times of Joe Louis Barrow, a.k.a. Joe Louis* (New York: E. P. Dutton, 1974); and Randy Roberts, *Joe Louis: Hard Times Man* (New Haven, CT: Yale University Press, 2012).

Chapter 3

Robert Peterson's *Only the Ball Was White: A History of Legendary Black Players and All-Black Professional Teams* (New York: Oxford University Press,

1970) was the early key account on its subject. Donn Rogosin's *Invisible Men: Life in Baseball's Negro Leagues* (New York: Atheneum, 1983) and Neil Lanctot's *Negro League Baseball: The Rise and Ruin of a Black Institution* (Philadelphia: University of Pennsylvania Press, 2004) are very good more recent additions. Roberta Newman and Joel Nathan Rosen, *Black Baseball, Black Business: Race Enterprise and the Fate of the Segregated Dollar* (Jackson: University Press of Mississippi, 2014), offers a focused examination of the business side of the Negro Leagues.

Important biographies of Negro Leaguers include Larry Tye, *Satchel: The Life and Times of an American Legend* (New York: Random House, 2009); William Brashler, *Josh Gibson: A Life in the Negro Leagues* (Chicago: Ivan R. Dee, 2000); and John B. Holway, *Josh and Satch: The Life and Times of Josh Gibson and Satchel Paige* (Westport, CT: Meckler, 1991).

Chapter 4

On Branch Rickey, see Lee Lowenfish, *Branch Rickey: Baseball's Ferocious Gentleman* (Lincoln: University of Nebraska Press, 2007); Murray Polner, *Branch Rickey: A Biography* (New York: Atheneum, 1982); Harvey Frommer, *Rickey and Robinson: The Men Who Broke Baseball's Color Barrier* (New York: Macmillan, 1982); and David Lipman, *Mr. Baseball: The Story of Branch Rickey* (New York: G. P. Putnam's Sons, 1966). Stephen Fox's "The Education of Branch Rickey" in *Civilization* (September/October 1995) is a very good review of the complexities of Rickey's evolution on race.

Two books provide personal insights on the storied Dodgers franchise: Peter Golenbock, *Bums: An Oral History of the Brooklyn Dodgers* (New York: G. P. Putnam's Sons, 1984) and Roger Kahn, *The Boys of Summer* (New York: Harper and Row, 1971). Chris Lamb's *Blackout: The Untold Story of Jackie Robinson's First Spring Training* (Lincoln: University of Nebraska Press, 2004) sheds light on Robinson's first entry into the Dodgers system.

Chapter 5

Jonathan Eig's *Opening Day: The Story of Jackie Robinson's First Season* (New York: Simon and Schuster, 2007) is a helpful examination of the year that Robinson broke into the Majors. Red Barber, *1947: When All Hell Broke Loose in Baseball* (New York: Da Capo Press, 1982) and Roy Campanella, *It's Good to Be Alive* (Lincoln: University of Nebraska Press, 1995) provide additional color on the Dodgers.

Chapter 6

On Paul Robeson, Martin Baum Duberman, *Paul Robeson* (New York: Alfred A. Knopf, 1988) remains an important book. Also helpful are Acklyn R. Lynch, "Paul Robeson: His Dreams Know No Frontiers," *Journal of Negro Education* 45, no. 3 (Summer 1976): 225–34; Darlene Clark Hine, "Paul Robeson's Impact on History," in *Paul Robeson: The Great Forerunner* (New York: International Publishers, 1998); Joseph Walwik, "Paul Robeson, Peekskill, and the Red Menace," *Pennsylvania History* 66, no. 1 (Winter 1999): 71–82; and Mary E. Cygan, "A Man of His Times: Paul Robeson and the Press, 1924–1976," *Pennsylvania History* 66, no. 1 (Winter 1999): 27–46.

Thomas Sugrue's *Sweet Land of Liberty: The Forgotten Struggle for Civil Rights in the North* (New York: Random House, 2008) provides important context for Robeson's African American activism in the period before the Civil Rights Movement.

Chapters 7 and 8

On 1960s party politics, Steven F. Lawson, *Running for Freedom: Civil Rights and Black Politics in American Since 1941*, 2nd edition (New York: McGraw Hill, 1997) provides a good overview. Theodore White's old standard, *The Making of the President 1964* (New York: Atheneum Publishers, 1965) still contributes important and colorful detail, and Rick Perlstein's *Nixonland: The Rise of a President and the Fracturing of America* (New York: Scribner, 2009) is the most recent of many important studies of Nixon's impact. See Richard Norton Smith's *On His Own Terms: A Life of Nelson Rockefeller* (New York: Random House, 2014) for a thorough examination of its subject.

The literature on the African American freedom struggle is vast. Martha Biondi, *To Stand and Fight: The Struggle for Civil Rights in Postwar New York City* (Cambridge: Harvard University Press, 2006) gives a particular look at Robinson's region that is helpful here. Among the growing literature on the Black Power period, Peniel Joseph, *Waiting 'Til the Midnight Hour: A Narrative History of Black Power in America* (New York: Owl Books, 2006) and William L. Van Deburg, *New Day in Babylon: The Black Power Movement and American Culture, 1965–1975* (Chicago: University of Chicago Press, 1992) are especially instructive.

Index

About the Author

Born and raised in New Orleans, **J. Christopher Schutz** spent several years in California doing community work, including at an AIDS agency, a food bank, and as a juvenile hall chaplain in the Oakland area. The issues he encountered in those years formulated the questions he sought to explore as he entered graduate school studies, earning a master's degree at the University of North Carolina-Charlotte and a Ph.D. at the University of Georgia.

Specializing in the study of race and Southern history as well as social and cultural history in post-World War II America, Schutz is currently completing a study of the 1972 Charlotte Three case (which targeted Black Power activists in North Carolina). He is professor of history at Tennessee Wesleyan College.